T0150434

# Brigadistes

"An extraordinary book. Perceptively written, beautifully translated and accompanied by wonderful photographs, it brings us close to the heroism and sacrifices of those who risked their lives in the fight against fascism."
—Paul Preston, author of *The Spanish Civil War: Reaction, Revolution and Revenge*

"A beautiful, touching tribute to the everyday heroes who battled so bravely in the fight against fascism."
—Maxine Peake, actor

"A real treasure that we can't stop exploring."
—*La Republica*

"Real and very human ... Reliving these lives, today, is more important than ever."
—*Cazarabet*

"Told with skill, sensitivity and rigor, [...] these are the stories that Jordi Marti-Rueda has been collecting for years. They fought for ideals in a battle against fascism – a global threat that remains to this day."
—*El Temps*

"An excellent introduction to the world of the International Brigades."
—*AB Origine*

"Brings us close to the most human face of war."
—*El Salto*

# Brigadistes
## Lives for Liberty

Jordi Martí-Rueda

Translated from Catalan by Mary Ann Newman

Foreword by Jordi Borràs

First published in 2020 in the Catalan language as *Brigadistes: Vides per la llibertat* by Tigre de Paper Edicions

English language edition first published 2022 by Pluto Press
New Wing, Somerset House, Strand, London WC2R 1LA

www.plutobooks.com

This English edition of *Brigadistes* was arranged via Red Rock Literary Agency Ltd and Oh! Books Literary Agency

The translation of this work has been supported by the Institut Ramon Llull

**LLLL** institut
ramon llull

Copyright © Jordi Martí-Rueda 2020 in agreement with Tigre de Paper Edicions
English language translation copyright © Mary Ann Newman 2022

The right of Jordi Martí-Rueda to be identified as the author of this work has been asserted in accordance with the Copyright, Designs and Patents Act 1988.

British Library Cataloguing in Publication Data
A catalogue record for this book is available from the British Library

ISBN  978 0 7453 4712 7  Paperback
ISBN  978 0 7453 4738 7  PDF
ISBN  978 0 7453 4713 4  EPUB eBook

This book is printed on paper suitable for recycling and made from fully managed and sustained forest sources. Logging, pulping and manufacturing processes are expected to conform to the environmental standards of the country of origin.

Typeset by Stanford DTP Services, Northampton, England

Simultaneously printed in the United Kingdom and United States of America

For my parents, Joan and Fina, for filling me to the brim.
For Judit and Roger, the salt of my life.

# Contents

# Foreword

*Jordi Borràs*

The Baron's vineyard was located at the foot of the Pàndols mountains, right next door to my childhood home. As children, we would play in those vineyards, and the past would always surface among the clumps of earth we threw at each other in our war play. From the compacted earth would emerge scraps of shrapnel, tins of food, or shell casings from the bullets of the war—the real war—that had butchered the region decades before. We barely had to scratch the surface for things to show up, including the bones of nameless soldiers whom no one had come to claim. It was the 1980s and the silence of a never-healed wound still floated over the village. Every so often, when we found a clip loaded with bullets, we would spend hours cleaning the rim of the cartridge by rubbing it over and over with a finger coated in spit. Little by little, the mud encrusted over half a century would vanish and, as if by magic, the year and the letters revealing its origin would appear. By the age of ten, we could already deduce which side any given bullet belonged to. We were thrilled when we found a special one, and everyone would run over to observe it like a treasure and guess at its provenance. The international footprint was patent in that little corner of the Baron's vineyard, where Russian or American bullets might appear, as well as remnants of Italian grenades and scraps of shrapnel from Italian or German mortars. If you were paying attention, and took the time to read some of the engraved stones scattered in different corners of the village, the footprints of those soldiers who spoke strange languages could be seen everywhere. From the gravestone of the Nazi aviator that lay for years in a corner by the *Escoles Velles* (Old Schools), to the plaque in the cemetery in memory of a brigadista from the Lincoln Battalion, who had died in combat at only twenty-two. The wound, always the wound. As children, those things led us to imagine war stories and their heroes, many of whom came from all over the world to combat the fascist monster that had used our land as its battlefield and as the training ground of a worldwide conflict that would soon leave Europe in ruins. Our grandparents from the villages of the Pàndols and Cavalls mountains had also been there at the Battle of the Ebre River. We pictured them fighting side by side with those noble and valiant young men who had left everything behind to take on the risks of a distant war.

What you will find in this book is precisely the noble spirit of those men and women who put their bodies in the path of fascist hatred. Many of those brigadistes came to our homeland with nothing to their names, with no other baggage than the impetus of their ideals, crossing Europe by bicycle or the Atlantic by ship, all uncertain as to whether they would return alive from beyond the Pyrenees. It was here where many of them infused words like liberty, solidarity, camaraderie, and anti-fascism with dignity. But they came to know other words, like terror, hatred, and death, as they were inscribed on their very own flesh. Words that mowed down the hopes, paths, and lives of many of those youths who threw themselves into the war against the triple Nazi-Fascist alliance of the troops commanded by Franco, Hitler, and Mussolini.

*Brigadistes: Lives for Liberty* is a book of literary and photographic portraits, sixty profiles accompanied by photographs that help us form a more precise sense of these characters. Written with impeccable style, these are true, poignant stories, as deeply powerful as the conviction that led their protagonists to take up their rifles in rocky trenches or drive ambulances as they dodged mortars in a country that was not their own. The brevity of the stories allows our imaginations to soar. To stop and take a breath between pages as we absorb these incredible stories, trying to rush beyond the limits of what is written to fill in the stories of lives deserving of a novel, of a widescreen movie, with popcorn in hand and eyes wide open with astonishment.

These sixty portraits could be sixty volumes of memories of a series of characters who gave their all for freedom.

But eighty years after the end of the Spanish Civil War there are still those who would have us believe that books like the one you hold in your hands are a thing of the past; that the war came to an end, and Franco died, and Nazi-Fascism is nothing but an old memory to fill encyclopedias; and that the wound has long been cauterized, as if by magic, as a result of the transition to democracy sealed by the Pact of 1978. They are the same people who would have us believe that it's better not to muddy the waters, for fear of something like what happened when we picked up the clumps of earth in the Baron's vineyard—buried today under bricks, asphalt, and cement. For with very little effort, the land could regurgitate history, spitting out memories buried in the shape of shrapnel and the bones of soldiers hidden by the fallacy of the Spanish Transition to Democracy. This is why I am so certain that *Brigadistes: Lives for Liberty* speaks not only of the past, but also of an uneasy present that trains a mirror on the shame and silences of some, while reminding us of the danger we court if amnesia takes hold. It is no secret that, if we are not capable of understanding our own history, we will be condemned to repeat it. Let us read, then, because there is no greater vaccination against the virus of fascism than the knowledge of a past that should be more present than ever.

# Acknowledgments

Many have participated in the photographic research for this book, and I would like to thank them here. First of all, the publisher, for their valuable aid. And, needless to say, I wish to thank those who have generously either provided photographs themselves or made it possible to obtain them: the Asociación de Amigos de las Brigadas Internacionales (Association of Friends of the International Brigades), Pere Audí, Richard Baxell, Eugènia Broggi and family, The Center for Documentation of the International Brigades, Jordi Creus, Peter Crome, Megan Dobney, Alfonso Domingo, Christine Dyger, Sebastiaan Faber, Crispin Green and Frances Green, Mariado Hinojosa, Máximo Iaffa, Meirian Jump, David Lowe, Sylvia Martin, Manus O'Riordan, Miquel Perelló Segura, Mireia Sentís, Jordi Torrent, Eddie Tyrone, Caterina Úbeda, Peter Verburgh, Alan Warren, and Stuart Walsh.

# Translator's Preface

*Brigadistes: Lives for Liberty* is a sampler of men and women from all over the world who gather in Spain to try to face fascism down. The book is written in Catalan and, though the action takes place all over the Iberian Peninsula, its emotional capital, and the erstwhile capital of the Spanish Republic, is Barcelona.

English-language readers of Spanish Civil War literature may be accustomed to seeing relevant toponyms and military terms written in Spanish. In *Brigadistes*, we have honored the source language and rendered these terms in Catalan. For example, in Catalan, as in Spanish, *brigadista* is the singular term for a member of the Brigades, but the Catalan plural is *brigadistes*, hence the final "-es."

However, when dealing with place names, we have hewn to the map: if the site of a battle or hospital is in Catalonia, the toponym is in Catalan; if it is in Castile or Andalusia, it is in Spanish. For example, the chapter titled "Erika Glaser" includes a sentence about her father, Willy Glaser, who had "worked in hospitals in Castilla-La Mancha and Alacant." Castilla-La Mancha is a Spanish-speaking region, so the toponym is in Spanish; Alacant is a province in the Valencian Community, and hence the toponym is in Catalan, as is Ebre, the river that gives its name to one of the longest, bloodiest battles of the Civil War.

Among the foreign actors who influenced or took part in the war was the Comintern, the Communist International, which supported the cause of the Spanish Republic while in fact also exerting Soviet control over policy decisions on the battleground, as can be seen in the chapter titled "Len Crome."

In contrast, the following chapter, about Argentine Brigadista, Capitana Mika Etchebéhère, mentions the POUM, the Partit Obrer Unificat Marxista (Workers' Party of Marxist Unification), an anti-Soviet communist formation founded by Joaquín

Maurín and Andreu Nin. This is the group with which George Orwell was affiliated, featured in *Homage to Catalonia*.

Mention is also made of the Non-Intervention Committee, arranged, at the outset, by the French and British governments and eventually joined by twenty-seven nations, which, ironically, included Italy, Germany, and the Soviet Union. This Committee evinced neutrality to avoid expansion of the war, but in fact choked the Spanish Republic by essentially establishing an embargo, tipping the balance toward Franco's Nationalist uprising, which received abundant support from Mussolini and Hitler.

*Brigadistes: Lives for Liberty* is rich in historical references, some of which are familiar, others of which will be less identifiable, but this assembly of heroic and often tragic personalities makes these nuances of early twentieth-century history accessible to all readers.

*Mary Ann Newman*
New York, November 2021

# Introduction: Living and Reliving

I have often imagined a first encounter with the enigmatic English captain. A sort of formal introduction to the character. I have read so many stories that my imagination has elaborated, unwittingly, a sort of cinematographic traveling shot following the man's steps for the first time.

It is December and, on the outskirts of the town, amid the fields of La Mancha, the world is divided equally into land and sky—an endless blue in which a glassy sun hangs. To the left and to the right, the dry fields stretch until they merge with the sky. In the foreground, the four stone houses seem to prefer huddling together against the wind to blocking its path.

Accustomed to Irish winters, Frank doesn't seem put out. He hasn't even bothered to zip up his jacket. I slip into place by his side. "Poor Frank," I think. "The great Irishman, the hero of Limerick. A whole life against the British, and here they saddle him with an English captain. An irony of fate if I've ever seen one, hey, Frank? Worthy of a malicious screenwriter."

Frank doesn't notice my presence—neither he nor the handful of Irishmen beside him. They only have eyes for the man before them, far more interesting than me. I, too, look in his direction. It's hard to understand what he's saying because the wind carries his words off. Even so, he cuts a commanding figure. He bears no resemblance to the boys who have landed in this corner of La Mancha from the slums of London, Liverpool, and Dublin. It is not that George Nathan, as this is his name, is wearing more distinguished clothing. He, too, is wearing an old woolen sweater, pants dirty with dust, and worn-out leather shoes. But there is something that sets him apart.

He is tall and lean, with an aristocratic grace. His face is rather long and his nose seigniorial, touched off with a thin moustache, carefully trimmed as if it were a precious jewel. He holds a pipe

1

in his mouth, which gives him an air of distinction, and when he speaks he accompanies his words with an elegant gesture. As his voice is clipped by the wind, only syllables and fragments of words reach us, but they sound crystalline, enunciated with Shakespearean precision.

"Maybe that's it," I think. "Maybe this is why Frank is so riveted." The contrast between the plainness of the clothing and the majestic air of the man wearing them. "A man of refinement dressed in garments that do not befit him. A romantic gentleman whom the novelist has placed in the wrong scene."

Frank is still scrutinizing George Nathan's face, his expressions, his speech, as if he wanted to decipher him. Beyond the fields framing the English captain, the four stone houses cower on the ground and the bell tower soars too high for so little a village.

And when the scene comes to an end, I confess that I do not know if the first encounter between these two personalities actually went like that. The man Frank Ryan regarded, or observed in a memory composed of fragments, was a character fit for a novel.

When the day to enter into combat arrived, his appearance had undergone a deep change. The London, Liverpool, and Dublin boys fell silent. He stood before them decked out in the uniform of the British Army, wearing an officer's high boots, shined to a brilliant finish. A whistle graced his lips and he brandished an old-fashioned lord's walking stick, as if he were a captain in an ancient war. His whole life had groomed him for this day.

From that moment on, each of George Nathan's gestures would enhance this image. He walked through enemy fire as a romantic hero or a corsair from an Emilio Salgari novel might do. Tall and erect, indifferent to bullets, he led attacks and called his men to retreat to the sound of his whistle, mocking the enemy and cracking jokes to undo the thundering of the bombs. His temerity became the stuff of legend and was a balm to the boys who found themselves under fire for the first time. True to

English custom, at lunch or teatime, he would sit down to a table set with clean linens even as mortar fire rained down.

No one knew much about him. They all knew he wasn't a communist, and he seemed to have no more ideology than the desire to combat fascism. Everyone knew he was homosexual and even though in the 1930s that was practically a crime, when it came to George Nathan, it didn't seem to matter to anyone. Fanciful rumors circulated about his past life and his reasons for going to war. It was said that he had served in Her Majesty's Guard, that he had refused to obey the order to open fire on British strikers, that he had torn up his uniform, that he had embarked for America, that he had lived like a vagabond, that he had become an impoverished laborer.

The biggest secret, though, exploded in the first days of 1937, when a grim rumor surfaced. It was said that, years before, during the Irish War of Independence, Nathan had formed part of an irregular company, organized by the British Government, which had fought the IRA activists and the population that sheltered them. The company in question were the Black and Tans, who had left a fateful memory in Irish homes everywhere.

The news almost caused an Irish revolt at the International Brigades base, and the old English captain was finally obliged to address the issue before an assembly of Irishmen. As for what was said, we have only the recollection of one of the men present. George Nathan admitted that he had served in the intelligence unit in the county of Limerick, the land of Frank Ryan. He also told them that he had matured, that they had all matured, and that now they were facing a common enemy who had to be defeated. Some of the Irish soldiers did not want to fight under the orders of someone who had been their parents' worst enemy in the past. Others, however, accepted his words; these were the men who, not incidentally, had come to know him under fire. The ones who had shared with him the experience of dodging bullets and mortar shells on the Jaén and Madrid fronts. And they had concluded that, if they had to confront the mechanized armies of Franco, Hitler, and Mussolini, the best way to do it was by that captain's side.

This is surely the greatest of the paradoxes associated with Nathan. Both that from their very first battles he had learned to admire the daring of the Irish soldiers; and that they, former IRA combatants, had come to regard him with warmth and affection.

Frank Ryan and George Nathan: impossible to find two more antithetical characters in those spheres. But the war of 1936 is fertile ground for irony because it attracted forty thousand souls from every continent, forty thousand stories, and forty thousand sensibilities, and placed them all in the same trench. Most of them formed part of the International Brigades; others, the Antifascist Militias or other units of the Republican army.

What you have here is a few of those stories gathered under the title "Brigadistes," even if not every protagonist belonged to the International Brigades. Sixty flashes of light, sixty brushstrokes, conjoined by one sole need and desire: to fight fascism and defeat it before it was too late. And today it is imperative to relive them.

The Bravest Woman
in Barcelona

Fanny Schoonheyt couldn't understand how she had not been killed on the very first day. The army had spread through the streets of Barcelona and the city had hurled itself full bore upon the soldiers. She had not had time to change her clothes for the event. The *coup d'état* had surprised her wearing a yellow blouse and as the people stormed the barracks she felt her whole person was a luminous target. She concluded that the sight of a blonde girl wearing a yellow blouse scaling the roofs of the barracks must have made such an impression on the soldiers that they hadn't had time to take aim and fire.

Fanny had had a job on a Rotterdam daily newspaper, but she had not managed to realize her dream of becoming part of the editorial staff, a stronghold reserved for men. In the end, she had left her native Holland, which seemed flat and boring to her, and taken up residence in Barcelona, the least boring city in Europe, the refuge of Germans who had fled Nazism and a bubbling cultural cauldron.

A short time after the coup, she left for the Aragon front. The International Brigades didn't yet exist, but she didn't even consider waiting. She got her hands on a machine gun and didn't let go of it until she was wounded. The press showered praise on her. They christened her the machine gun queen and the bravest woman in Barcelona, and one journalist described her eyes as the reflection of a Nordic lake. "Foolishness," she replied. She hated to talk about herself or to be talked about, even more so if it was to make metaphors about her eyes. One of the people who came to know her was Marina Ginestà. She was the *miliciana*, the militiawoman, who was immortalized in an iconic photograph from the first days of the war in revolutionary Barcelona: a young woman on a rooftop with the city at her feet, a rifle hanging from her shoulder and a shock of hair ruffled by the breeze, smiling for the camera. Maria Ginestà said of Fanny that it was hard not to look at her.[1] Because she was tall and blonde. And she smoked cigarettes. And because she did it unselfconsciously, at a time when in Barcelona no woman dared to light up a cigarette in public.

Painter and Miliciana

In a letter to a friend, Felicia Browne wrote to say that painting and sculpture were her life, but that she would abandon them if a greater cause demanded it. And that is what she did. A short time before the fascist coup d'état, she traveled from England to Barcelona to experience the People's Olympiad from close up. What she experienced instead was the outbreak of the Spanish Civil War and fighting in the streets. They didn't accept her in the medical corps, so she showed up in the offices of the Partit Socialista Unificat de Catalunya (PSUC—the Catalan Communist Party) to sign up for the militia. True to her word, she went straight to the Aragon front, carrying paper and charcoal pencils in her knapsack, and a rifle on her back.

It was not the first time she had faced fascism. Felicia had been born into a well-to-do family on the outskirts of London and had studied at a good art school. But later, while studying sculpture in Germany, uneasiness had filtered into the classrooms. She had seen how fascism was growing and slipping through the cracks, how the Hitler Youth showed off their uniforms and the voice of Hitler spread throughout the country. That was when she turned her gaze from plaster and stone sculptures and joined the first struggles against the Nazis on the streets of Berlin.

Near Tardienta, a month after the war broke out, she tried to help a wounded Italian friend. Both of them died under machine gun fire. A short time later, the British press announced the death of a young English woman, the first person from Great Britain to die in the war. Her fellow soldiers salvaged the drawings she had done in the weeks she spent in Barcelona and on the front. They were portraits of militiamen and women, and Aragonese peasants, figures with the vitality of the swift line of an ephemeral draft. If she had not stopped to help her Italian friend, perhaps they would have come to be paintings, on the day that art once again took up its rightful place in the life of Felicia Browne.

The Nielsen Brothers

In August 1936, a short time after the war broke out, the Nielsen brothers, Harald, Kai, and Aage, bade farewell to their parents and friends, and to their fellow laborers at the factory where they worked. They got on their three bicycles and, with another friend for company, they started pedaling. They rode through Copenhagen, crossed Europe from north to south, and, in a few weeks, arrived in the Iberian Peninsula.

Before the creation of the International Brigades and before the Communist International began to spread the word that volunteers were needed and organize trips to the Peninsula from all over the world, anyone who wanted to fight fascism had to find their own way and pay out of their own pocket for the trip, assume the risks of crossing a Europe that had become dangerous, and convince the Spanish Republican authorities to allow them to join their ranks. Who knows what became of those bicycles? What we do know of the three brothers is that they signed up with the Thaelmann Brigade, alongside other Scandinavians, German, Austrians, and Swiss, and they joined the struggle to save Madrid.

One photograph shows them in August 1936, pedaling over the Lillebaeltsbroen (Little Belt Bridge, in Denmark), intent on reaching the Peninsula. During the war, there are shots showing the three of them together in a break between battles. In the fall of 1936, a short time after they arrived, they appear in uniform, their blankets slung across their chests, smiling for the camera. Smoking a cigarette in the grass on the Madrid front. Or reading a newspaper on the Guadalajara front.

Few of the volunteers who arrived in those first days had not been carried off by death by war's end. Miraculously, the three Nielsens all returned home. But, by 1939, as they had feared, the European landscape had darkened. In Denmark, they were awaited by the Nazis and the collaborationists. And also the Resistance. And more war. And, finally, for the youngest of them, the Grim Reaper.

Welcome to the War,
Penny Phelps

Accustomed to the ash-gray sky of London, the first thing that struck Penny Phelps when she reached Portbou was the sunlight. The sharp, biting blue of the Mediterranean. Aboard the train, she seeks it out from the windows of the car, among the heads bobbing with the movement of the train. She is twenty-seven years old and it is the first time she has left England. With her are two other girls, but the rest of the train is filled with young men in uniform, bearing arms that seem too big for them.

Her fellow travelers do not seem at all disturbed at the idea of going to the front. They are chatting happily, and vociferously, and they smile at her.

"*Inglesa,*" "*enfermera,*" she responds, "English," "nurse," because it is all she knows how to say.

The train stops at every station and through the windows come oranges, chunks of bread, and wine, gifts bestowed on the travelers by anonymous creased hands. The soldiers insist on sharing their lunch with the nurses. A wineskin makes the rounds of the train car, from hand to hand and from mouth to mouth. It doesn't seem like a very sanitary habit, and Penny Phelps hopes to herself that the wineskin won't reach her part of the train. But arrive it does, from hand to hand, and from mouth to mouth. She bows her head and examines her shoes, but she can hear the gulps and the laughter coming closer and closer. She prays that some redeeming hand will deflect the path of that filthy receptacle, but to no avail. No redeeming hand carries off the wineskin, which advances inexorably toward her, and, when she foolishly lifts her head, she finds it right in front of her, in the hand of a young soldier, who offers it to her, with a smile, of course. Penny Phelps looks at the vessel. It is made of leather, it is wet, and it has been manhandled by every set of hands in the car. Her fingers touch the wet leather. She tries to hide her disgust and she forces a smile. She closes her eyes and opens her lips. A harsh liquid lands on her tongue and burns her throat. Welcome to the war, Penny Phelps.

The Long March

The crest of the Pyrenees was outlined in the darkness like a line of insurmountable battlements. Jimmy Yates knew that before the sun peeked out he would be on the other side, in the Catalonia of the Republic. Others had followed this path before him. Two generations before, on the day slavery was abolished, his grandmother had danced madly through the streets. But he had grown up in a Mississippi town where every day the dawn revealed black bodies dangling from the branches of the trees. The day he fled for Chicago he put his cotton factory uniform on over his traveling clothes. "You look fatter every day," his mother had said. "You're imagining things," he responded, and he left without finding the courage to tell her that he would not be home for supper.[2] The soldiers' feet dance on the wet grass. They had been issued *espardenyes*, hemp sandals, so the sound of their feet wouldn't tip off the patrols of the Non-Intervention Committee that riddled the mountains. He was bathed in sweat and his legs trembled. He opened his pack and took out one of his three books. It didn't matter which one. He left it in the grass. When he had reached Chicago, he was afraid to ease his thirst at a public fountain because in the world he came from that would mean that the following day his body would be hanging from a tree. The wind whipped through his clothing, it nipped at the edges of his eyes, it pierced his skin. Each step he took wore him down a little more. He opened his bindle. He didn't want to look. A second book would have to die so the third could be saved. As a child, to learn to read he had had to walk sixteen kilometers to the school for Black children. He had learned each letter sitting on a wooden bench. Every hilltop they climbed heralded the next. They walked down the hills, then up. They tripped. They cried in silence. Their bodies doubled over and gave up. He opened the bindle for the last time. He looked at the book. He saw the poems of Langston Hughes, the poet of Harlem. He ran his fingers over the edges. He chose a stone. He placed it there with care. He stood back up. The silhouette of the mountain crest appeared against a lilac canvas.

The Nurse from Harlem

In the life she dreamed of as a little girl, she would be a physical education teacher. But it was just a dream. Because, in the United States, the hygiene laws did not allow Black people to swim in university pools or major in physical education. She got her nursing degree at the Harlem Hospital School of Nursing and, in 1935, she wanted to travel to Ethiopia to nurse the civilian population that was being shelled by Mussolini's planes. This, too, was impossible. The New York office of the Red Cross refused her services because the color of her skin made it impossible for her to serve in the name of the institution—even if it was in Africa.

We never know what lies behind a closing door nor what awaits us behind one that opens. When she embarked on the *S.S. Paris*, from the New York docks, Salaria Kea never imagined that what awaited her on the Iberian Peninsula was something much like utopia; for fourteen months of her life, the fourteen months that she would serve in the Civil War, no one would look at the color of her skin before deciding if she was a good person or a good nurse.

On April 3, 1937, she was greeted by the white houses of Portbou and the blue of the Mediterranean. The entire town had crowded into the station to welcome the group of doctors and nurses who were arriving from the United States. A little boy wriggled out of the group and ran toward her. He must have been around ten. He grabbed her by the hand and spoke to her in a language she didn't understand. They translated his words for her. He had lost his parents and a brother in the last bombing, and he was asking her to stay, to suspend the rest of her trip, because then she could care for them when the bombs fell again. She knew this was impossible. Her destination was at the front, where men were dying by the thousands. She boarded the train, anxious to arrive. But on the road south, as the coastal towns flew by the window overlooking the sea, she could still feel, and all her life she would feel, the words of those five fingers in her hand.

The Road

News of the uprising spread throughout Europe, penetrating the walls of a Hungarian prison and filtering through the bars of the cell of István Bakallár. When he got out he was twenty-three years old and his pockets were empty. He was under police surveillance for subversive activities and he couldn't get a passport. He packed everything he had into a bindle. His girlfriend tried to talk sense into him but, in the end, she prepared him a package of meat and crackers for the trip. From a telephone at the station, he spent one of his three coins, and amid the noise of the trains he said goodbye to her one more time. So she would think he was traveling by train. It was early summer.

He walked down roads. He hid in a wagon to hitch a ride until the owner awakened him with a whipping. He slept under a mantle of cornhusks. He fled from Hungary through the forests. He slept in the houses of Austrian farmers. Since they hated the Nazis, he would confess to them where he was going, and they asked him to write to them from Spain. He promised he would. He crossed another border. He jumped off a moving train to give Mussolini's police the slip. They captured him. They shut him up in the prison at Brunico. He went on a hunger strike so they would let him go. He got out three weeks later and collapsed in the street. They sent him back to the Austrian border. He shaved and bathed in a river. He started walking, but his legs couldn't hold him up. He ran into two lone boys picking pears from a tree. They were Hungarian, too, and they were even worse off than he. He gave one of them a shirt and the other a sock. They got as far as Switzerland in a train car carpeted with horse excrement. They made it to Paris. The French Communist Party helped them get as far as the Pyrenees. They crossed the mountain peak at night, with dozens of men like them. As the sun's fingers touched the horizon, they crossed the border. He only knew it because the guide came to a halt. He shouted, "Rest here." István Bakallár fell asleep on the rocks. It was the end of the summer.

The Enemy

"Bolshevik pig, you're not even worth a bullet," the SS commandant spat at him. There were two ways to die in Dachau: torture or suicide. And Hans Beimler had rejected the second option. He had been a communist deputy in the Reichstag until Hitler burned the parliament down and the great persecution began.

The Nazis weren't content just to see him die. They wanted to savor his defeat, his renunciation of life. But he had not touched the knife they left in his cell, or the two-meter rope with which to hang himself. Fed up with seeing him alive, they hauled him out of his cell and tossed him into a friend's cell. He found his friend's dead body lying on the ground, rotting and disfigured after four days. He covered his eyes. When they took him back to his own cell, the commandant had hung the cord from a pipe and made a slip-knot. All he had to do was get up on his cot, put his head in the noose, and let his body drop. That was it. He had two hours, until five p.m., to do it. Not today, he responded. It was his son's birthday, and he didn't want it to be a day of sadness for the rest of his life. The guard allowed him a few more hours, till seven in the morning. If he opened the door to find him alive at that hour, he would be sorry not to be dead. But Hans Beimler was smiling inside. He just needed to wait for nightfall. The following day his body was not hanging from the ceiling. It wasn't even in the cell. Maybe it was the locksmith's skills that his uncle had taught him when he was a boy. That last night he had opened the door to his cell and strangled the SS guard on watch.

In August 1936, we find him in Barcelona. He has organized a group of German refugees, which he christens with the name Ernst Thaelmann, in honor of a friend imprisoned by the Nazis, as he prepares to fight their common enemy and to perform once more the story of his life on a new stage.

César Covo

Not even the greatest literature can do justice to what happened there, wrote Juan Miguel de Mora of Mexico. But some words have the power to bestow voice and sight on the deaf and the blind.

César Covo was the very image of the immigrant spirit that pervaded the International Brigades. He was born in Sofia, the capital of Bulgaria, in the heart of a Sephardic Jewish family. He was the grandson of a rabbi, but he had immigrated to France and become a member of the Communist Party. He reached the Iberian Peninsula in October 1936, and what he saw there can be corroborated hands down by all his companions.

War is a machine that destroys human beings. Only when one found oneself immersed in it did such an obvious truth come into relief. It resembled nothing one had known before crossing the border of war. Accidents in city or countryside bore no resemblance to the brutality with which lead bullets tore soldiers' bodies apart. Weapons threatened their lives with an atrocity that none of them could have conceived of in their past lives.

César Covo was at the Cerro de los Ángeles, the Hill of Angels, near Madrid, in October 1936. It was there that he understood the devastating power of German shrapnel, mortar shells that exploded before they hit the ground, discharging a horizontal shower of metal fragments that mowed the men down at chest level. "We will attend the funeral ceremonies of our first dead," he wrote. *It is hard, when you are twenty years old, to contemplate this inert, already rigid, thing, with bloody hands clutching its breast, as if hoping, from beyond death, to trap the explosion of shrapnel that has ripped open its ribcage. We will avenge him, of course, but in the meantime we will lay him in this hole that his own body has opened up, dug only a bit deeper by his comrades... From this moment on we are no longer playing at being soldiers...*[3]

# The Bullet that Didn't Whistle

Théo Francos was the son of Castilian immigrants in France, who always felt that his true home was the land of his parents. One August night in 1936, he said goodbye to his mother, crossed the Saint-Esprit Bridge and boarded a train that would carry him off to war. Sitting by the window, he watched the lights of Bayonne grow small and fixed his eyes on the face of the clock of the cathedral so that it would be the last thing he saw of his city. That was when he knew that half of his body belonged to the city he saw fading away.

At the Madrid front, a short time before entering combat for the first time, his captain pronounced one of the most famous maxims of any war. "Don't worry about the bullets you hear. They will not touch you. The bullet coming for you is the one you do not hear." Both the whistles of projectiles that mowed friends down and the possibilities of being caught by a silent bullet began to multiply.

But fate would befall him in a different war. The Germans had readied their weapons and taken aim. An enormous grave gaped behind the thirty-five men, ready to swallow up their bodies. He didn't want the last thing he saw in life to be the soldiers who were to kill him. He turned his eyes to the sky. Within the blue, he found the face of his mother and the hands on the face of the cathedral clock. He heard the bullets that killed his mates, but not his own. He fell into the grave, like all the dead.

The following morning, two farmers realized that among the bodies an arm was moving. They removed his body and rushed him away to a hiding place. Théo Francos woke up in the house of those farmers. The insignia on his breast, now mangled, had deflected the path of the bullet, which had lodged between his heart and his aorta, in a spot too delicate for any doctor to dare extract it. And there it stayed. The bullet that hadn't whistled would grow old along with him.

The Girl With the Truck

"Perhaps you *could* drive an ambulance. But at night, in the dark, on a highway torn up by bombs, do you think you would be capable of fixing an engine or changing a flat tire?"

She was slight, sunny, she was a dancer, she was married, and she was a woman. She lowered her eyes and accepted the verdict. For a couple of hours, at least. A short time later, the staff saw her return to the recruitment office in New York, in a state of fury.

Evelyn Hutchins was the only North American woman to drive ambulances on the front lines. As it turned out, she did know how to fix engines and change tires. And also to drive down highways torn up by bombs and to avoid potholes and to prevent any of the four wheels from falling into one of the hollows because, if that were to happen, the ambulance could be caught in a trap and the jolting could kill the most gravely wounded. As it turned out, she could do it at night and with the headlights off, as indeed they almost always were, to avert the attacks of enemy planes, as she looked out for the potholes, picturing the four wheels in her head, and also at full speed so that no one would die before reaching the operating room. On dry nights or in the rain, on muddy gravel roads that twisted up and down hills on sharp turns behind whose darkness hid steep cliffs. In the event she might run into Francoists infiltrated in Republican territory, she had two grenades in the cabin and a pistol on her belt. No difficulty flustered her. An ambulance driver is an ambulance driver, she declared.

They said she smelled more of petrol than perfume. Both her mates and reporters were amused to find such a small, cheery woman at the wheel of such a large vehicle. Many treated her with affection and took pictures of her. Others didn't. Years later she would say that those who didn't were her true buddies.

**Words and Bullets**

"I've had a fabulous idea: I'm going to Spain, to the Spanish revolution," wrote Pablo de la Torriente Brau in August of 1936. "In Cuba there is a saying, like a popular song: 'You must see Spain before you die.' And that's where I'm going now, to the Spanish revolution, where today the anguish of the entire world's oppressed is pulsating. The idea exploded inside my head and from that moment on the great forest of my imagination is burning."[4]

Pablo de la Torriente Brau was a gracious soul and a compulsive optimist, convinced that the justice and the sweat of all the men and women who defended the Republic would prevail over the Italian tanks, and win the war. He had been born in Puerto Rico, he had grown up in Cuba, he had been in exile in New York, and, in the winter of 1936, he was at the Madrid front. He was a journalist and a poet, and he wrote chronicles of revolutionary Barcelona and of Madrid under siege. He had the gift of seduction, when he wrote and when he spoke. He was an officer of the Republican forces and he visited the trenches urging on the defenders of Madrid to resist the onslaughts and save the city. By day, he shot Mexican bullets and, by night, if there were no bullets, he shot words. Before traveling to the Peninsula, he could never have imagined that by night he would be using his gift to educate the enemy.

"Let the Cuban talk!" a faceless voice would shout from across the enemy lines. And, sheltered by the parapets, he would clear his throat and shoot. We will never know if any of his words hit their target. But when he had finished speaking, from the fascist lines every night the same melody would ring out, a blast of machine gun fire, and the bullets would once again scatter his words. The name Pablo de la Torriente would always be associated with verbs and verses. His own and those of others who wrote for him. Not long after he died on the front of Majadahonda, Miguel Hernández dedicated his "Second Elegy" to him, and many years later the guitar of Silvio Rodríguez would turn it into a song.

Even the Olives Are Bleeding

No matter what else he did, Charlie Donnelly was a writer. Every minute of the day. He was born in Dungannon, a town in Belfast West, and he had been studying at the university until they expelled him for being a communist. He used his three months in prison to write a book. When he went to the Peninsula, at twenty-three, he had already published two essays, two novels, and a few poems, and he left behind a half-finished biography of Irish hero James Connolly. Not even at the front did he stop writing.

On February 27, 1937, he recited a quasi-poem, unintentionally composing an iconic tale of the Battle of Jarama. He took refuge from enemy fire behind an olive tree, one of the few trees still standing amid the devastation, like a monument to incomprehension. The Lincoln Battalion was retreating. He gathered up a few olives from the foot of the tree, squeezed them with all his might, and let the juice dribble through his fingers. A nearby Canadian soldier heard what he whispered, perhaps only to himself:

"Even the olives are bleeding."

A short time later, a hail of bullets brought him down.

The night-time truce for each side to gather its dead, that sacred respect among enemies for the salvaging of the wounded and the honoring of the fallen, was a relic of remote times, a romantic notion from the tales of the Trojan War. On the disfigured skin of the Jarama valley, enemy fire erected a wall between the living and those who had fallen silent. It took Charlie Donnelly's mates four days to recover his body. Not long before, he had written a poem in which he spoke of the death he had seen in the war. "Body awaits the tolerance of crows," went the last verse. And now, he floated like a bird, as if the line of poetry had written his own end.

The Man Who Made History

As historian Peter Carroll tells it, the day on which the Abraham Lincoln Battalion first saw combat, on the Jarama, as enemy planes released some silvery objects, a soldier exclaimed, "They're leaflets!" The pamphlets hit the ground faster than expected and set off a chain of explosions that stunned everyone into silence. After a grave hush, the soldier commented: "Those were some powerful leaflets."[5]

The name of that soldier was Oliver Law and he had been a free man for only a few weeks. There is a reason for this. In the United States of the 1930s, a Black American could not sit in the same train car as a white American, nor sit at the same table, nor piss in the same bathroom, nor engage in conversation in plain daylight for fear that a cop would arrest him for violating public morality. But strange things happened in the territory of the Republic, such as a company made up of white and black Americans being under the command of a descendent of slaves. The unit was the Abraham Lincoln Battalion and he was the first African-American in history to be the commander of men of all colors, the same man who had commented days before on the notorious launching of the leaflets. He had been a construction worker and, in January 1937, he had arrived on the Peninsula wearing the halo of a heroic activist, forged in his long history as a trade unionist in Chicago.

In Brunete, he received the order to attack a fascist position that was far too well fortified. He ordered the attack and started out. The commissar, who had shared demonstrations, arrests, and beatings with him in the police stations of Chicago, tried to hold him back. He knew it was hopeless. Oliver Law would not confine himself to watching his men carry out his orders. After a few brief words, he ran toward his death. And, surely, as he ran, even as he obeyed an order and a duty that obligated him to run, he continued to be a free man.

Smiles

With her black jacket, leather gloves, and high boots, and the broad smile she bestowed on the camera, no one would have said that Anne Taft was a nurse in the full throes of war. You could say that the cameras loved her. They usually found her dressed in a white coat, but almost always with that fetching smile, as if she hadn't been working for forty-eight hours without a break and didn't hold the lives of hundreds of men in her hands.

She was from the Bronx. She had graduated from a Brooklyn nursing school and in January 1937, just after her twenty-fourth birthday, she took off with the first team of North American doctors and nurses who were setting off to aid the Republic.

In a few hours, she and her team converted an abandoned school into a hospital to care for the wounded on the Jarama front. She mopped the floors and the walls of the whole building, disinfected them, decided how the wards would be distributed, and filled them with surgical equipment and beds. In no time, a flood of ambulances began to arrive and the wounded were dropped off. Hundreds of them, day and night. The operations succeeded one another en masse, with no sense of rules or schedules. Outside the operating theaters, the nurses desperately inhaled the smoke of the Spanish cigarettes and the anti-tank fire, and went back to work. The only thing that kept them from fainting were the rows of wounded waiting to be operated on. There was no running water and they had to run and fill buckets at the well. There was no indoor heating either, and the icy fingers of winter penetrated doors and windows and embraced all the living beings they could find. Sometimes Anne Taft would jump from one foot to the other to beat the cold climbing up her legs. She saw clouds of steam rising from reclining bodies and open wounds. And she was surprised that, despite it all, most of the wounded were saved and some of the most gravely wounded even recovered quickly. "It seems as if the will to live," she wrote, "is stronger when one is fighting for a better world."[6]

The Nameless

Every warrior is familiar with the first day malaise. What they knew as life up to that point was a pile of uncertainties and truths, misfortunes and joys, all the things one knows from close up, but whatever those things were, they had nothing to do with battle. And suddenly they found themselves immersed in an order in which life might last no more than a second, where the ground was up and the sky was down, and the lead bullets turned them into miserable, insignificant beings. Some of them could not bear the sudden descent, the collapse of their senses and their thoughts. Some were able to deal with it better on the second day.

Let us add that they were faced with a devastating mechanized army and that, if they raised their heads, they could see the bellies of Hitler's and Mussolini's planes opening up. The cargo they dropped would lift the men from the ground, scattering them like chess pieces. Let us imagine that neither you nor yours can do a thing to protect your lives because there is not a single functioning machine gun. This is what happened to a group of hundreds of boys from all over Europe in December 1936. They were sent off to the Jaén front before they even had time to choose a name for the battalion. The brief life of this unit came to an end in Jaén, and it earned its sad fame as the *Sense Nom*, the Nameless Battalion.

Months later, the person responsible for the defective weapons crossed the border and returned to France. His name was Henri Dupré, and he was a member of *La Cagoule*, the French fascist movement. Perhaps it is exaggerated to ascribe so much merit to him, but he had infiltrated the International Brigades in order to perform sabotage, and he had boasted about it. Beyond any doubt, he was a good actor because he deceived everyone and earned the confidence of the commander-in-chief. Still, everything has its price. During the occupation, he collaborated with the Nazis and, after the liberation of France, he was arrested, judged, and condemned to death. The last thing he did in life was to corroborate that the rifles aimed at him were in perfect working order.

The Decision

What Mirko Markovics saw when he looked at the map spread out on the table was a chessboard. To open the path for a black pawn, the bishop had to advance and be killed by the white knight. The move was absurd, and it had one problem: the bishop represented all his men. Mirko Markovics was a Serb from Montenegro but, following the death of Oliver Law, he was in charge of the Lincoln-Washington Battalion in the Battle of Brunete. He had been an officer in the Red Army in the Soviet Union and a member of the Yugoslavian Communist Party, and he didn't need any lessons in discipline. But after hearing the order from the brigade commandant and transferring it onto the map, he looked at the battalion commissar with a stern expression. Since this man was also from the Balkans, they spoke in Serbo-Croatian. The commandant, who was German, didn't understand a word, but he picked up every gesture, the reproach in every syllable, the sharp angles of every word that the unit commander and his commissar aimed at each other. He ordered Mirko Markovics to speak English.

There was nothing strange in a brigadista's wanting to know the reason behind an order or questioning one he thought was wrong. But that day Mirko Markovics did what the laws of every war forbid you to do: he disobeyed the summary order of a superior. He told him that he would not send his men to a death as certain as it was senseless, that he would not carry hundreds of sterile deaths on his shoulders. Then and there, before the table and the map, they relieved him of his command. But disobeying an order in wartime is a crime with a high price. And Mirko Markovics was positioned like a tennis ball wobbling on the net.

The ball fell on the right side. He suffered no further punishment and the General Staff decided he had been right. An outcome that could have gone another way. That day, when he placed his life upon the net, Mirko Markovics saved many more.

Len Crome

Lazar Kromen was born in Latvia but he immigrated to Scotland to study medicine and never returned. The Latvian government declared him a deserter, because he had not fulfilled his military service, and Lazar Kromen changed his nationality and his name. From then on, he would be known as Leonard Crome.

During the Civil War, he worked as a doctor and he earned one of the highest ranks of the Republican Army. What he couldn't imagine was that he would also earn enemies. As the Ebre offensive was being planned, he wrote a letter explaining that the ambulances coming from Britain were not well equipped, and this was an obstacle to the class struggle of the workers against fascism, and he proposed better coordination with the foreign organizations that were giving aid. The complaint reached the highest echelons of the International Brigades, and the chief Commissar, the Frenchman André Marty, in Spain to represent the interests of the Communist International, replied with fury. He accused Len Crome of promoting a workers' discourse that contradicted the policy of the Communist Party and of adopting theories suggestive of Trotskyism and fascism, which in his estimation were indistinguishable. "One of the most disagreeable characteristics of life in the International Brigades were the frequent denunciations,"[7] Len Crome would write years later.

His existence might have been hanging from a thread. But for all the attempts to remove him, he continued to direct the medical services and he would be remembered as one of the most capable doctors of the Republic. He would even describe his days on the Peninsula as "a gloriously happy time."[8]

In contrast, fate would behave impeccably with the man who had pursued him. André Marty, hero of the Russian Revolution, commandant of the base of the International Brigades, and dyed-in-the-wool Stalinist, would be expelled from his own party. The message was categorical: if André Marty could be a victim of the purges, no communist anywhere could be sure of his position. An ironic denouement that George Orwell himself might have approved of.

Capitana Etchebéhère

Mika Etchebéhère, a daughter of Russian immigrants, left Argentina to travel with her husband through the revolutionary landscapes of Europe. After crossing half the continent, they ended up at the Madrid front, with a POUM militia unit.

Not so much as a month had gone by when they handed all her husband's belongings over to Mika Etchebéhère: his pistol, his militia carnet, his fountain pen, and a container of aspirin he always carried in his pocket. She didn't cry, but her hands trembled so violently that she couldn't hold the weapon they extended to her. Mika Etchebéhère didn't have any military training, nor did she want any. Still, after her husband's death, his mates chose her to be their commander. She became a *capitana*, the only female captain in the Republican army. And she, who didn't want to fight in the war, proved to be an audacious leader in combat. It was not the only paradox the war bestowed on her.

One day she felt a bit distressed on seeing two priests sitting on a bench, waiting. Shots had been fired at the people in the neighborhood during the uprising, and later rifles had been found in the church. "So, am I really true to my ideals?" she wrote years later. *This war and this revolution are mine. I have dreamed of them since childhood, when I heard the tales of the Russian revolutionaries escaping from Siberia and the Czarist prisons. To serve this cause, Hipólito and I have spurned the great lakes of Patagonia, we have cut short the flight of our love, we have accepted the blood that had to be shed, our own and that of others. How to explain, then, this ill-ease before two priests who will have to die or a lovely little chapel that will have to burn? I must accept this revolution I yearned for, I must accept it completely, I must not repudiate any part of it [...]. I must also erase my ingenuous adolescent image of the revolution ... I know I must ... But when the time comes to pick up the munitions and the dynamite at the switchman's guard house, I shall not walk in front of the priests.*[9]

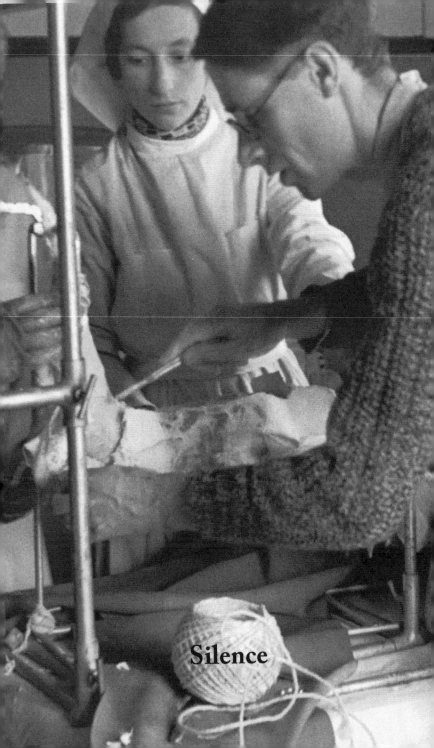

Silence

Dr. Moisès Broggi didn't know what war was. Nor did nurses Irene Goldin, Penny Phelps, or Thora Silverthorne. They thought hard about how to organize a hospital where the wounded would arrive in waves and there wasn't enough space to attend to all of them. They came up with ways to triage the most gravely wounded and they invented techniques that would save more lives than anyone could have imagined. Moisès Broggi gave thanks every day for the operating room nurse with whom he worked, Thora Silverthorne, of Wales. On the operating table, no instrument was ever lacking, she had a perfect command of sterilization techniques and, when his strength flagged, she would appear in the operating room with a pitcher of tea full to the brim. She had arrived in August 1936, with the first British volunteers. For her, abandoning the comforts of England had been a natural gesture. She had been a member of the Labour and Communist Parties, and while she was studying in Oxford and London, they had called her Thora the Red. During the Hunger Marches, she had bandaged the blisters on the strikers' feet. That August, at Victoria Station, before a cheering multitude that threw flowers at them, both at her and at the men, it had seemed an impossible dream that a few days later she would be on the Peninsula, with the Republicans. What would not seem natural was to leave.

Brunete put the organization and the resistance of nurses and doctors to the test. For almost a month, they fought against time in the triage rooms and the operating rooms, and they struggled with fatigue and exhaustion. But, suddenly, one day, the battle was over and silence fell upon the hospital. This overwhelmed Thora Silverthorne. When she tried to get up, she couldn't, and she let them carry her home. The doctors and nurses discovered that war had also wounded them. The wounds were not visible, but their muscles were frayed and they had lost the desire to speak. They had fallen to the bottom of a well and voices echoed down from the top of the shaft where the world was hiding.

The Patient

Ambulance drivers took great risks. In the daytime, they were attacked by Franco's planes and, at night, to avoid attack, they circulated without headlights, accepting the risk of tipping into a ravine or finding themselves in enemy territory. They zigzagged down highways disfigured by bombs. They moved with great care to avoid jolting that could kill the wounded and yet fast enough to get them to the hospitals alive. What else could add to the anxiety of those drivers? That some of their passengers would jump out of the moving truck and run back to the place where they had picked them up. They were deserters in reverse, who abandoned the places where they ought to be, not to flee from combat, but to return to it.

During the Battle of Brunete, one of the ambulances that took the wounded to the hospital of Villa Paz was carrying Walter Garland. He didn't jump out of the vehicle, but he turned out to be the worst patient the medical team had ever treated. He led a company of machine gunners, he felt responsible for them, and he couldn't bear to find himself lying in bed. Every day he begged them to let him return to the front, where his men were fighting while he rested between white sheets. None of the doctors would release him. Until his wounds had healed and his body had recovered enough to bear up under the harsh conditions of the trenches, the response would be no. The next day he would ask the same question, morning, noon, and night, and the nurses did what they could not to talk too much with him because they feared that their pleasantries would just be salt in the wound. Until one day the fascist planes strafed the hospital. While the attack was under way, no one paid any attention to Walter Garland's whereabouts. But when the nurses made the rounds in the evening, they found Garland's bed was empty—his and those of three other patients. The following day, still wearing their bandages, the four deserters greeted the ambulance drivers at the front.

Dr. Jolly

The ambulance would arrive, they would empty it out, it would take off, and, a short time later, it would come back full, even if the previous ambulance was not yet empty. The wounded arrived at the Tarancón hospital in delirious waves and, in the operating rooms, they worked as if on an assembly line. On one of the operating tables, the doctor wielded his scalpel with the speed of a samurai. His name was Douglas Jolly and he did his name proud. He had a robust and energetic constitution and he could operate all afternoon and through the night, the morning, the afternoon, and the following night. Penny Phelps had seen him work forty hours straight without a break, impervious to the cycle of time, like a monument to perseverance. As the hours passed, she would notice that Douglas Jolly's cheeks were getting red. It was his only sign of exhaustion. Despite his fatigue and the vibrations from the bombs, the scalpel was imperturbable in his fingers. Penny Phelps would describe him as one of the best surgeons she had ever worked with or would ever work with, and beyond any doubt the fastest.

He was from New Zealand, but the outbreak of the war had found him in London, where he was about to graduate. He knew that surgeons were needed in the Republican operating theaters, and he didn't wait to receive a diploma with his name on it. The energy in his body and the speed of his fingers were his contribution to the silent heroism of the Republican doctors and nurses. Another contribution was the gift of making people laugh when no one felt like laughing. They say that one day the medical team was waiting to be transported to the front. They were afraid that the enemy planes would show up while they were waiting, and everyone had fallen silent. Then Dr. Jolly broke the silence. He told a joke. Then another, and another, until they were all belly laughing—everyone except the Spanish doctors and nurses, who didn't understand a word. When he realized it, he stopped telling jokes, cleared his throat, and the entire medical team watched as he sang and performed a Maori dance.

George Nathan's Last Wish

"Steve, you old scoundrel!" roared George Nathan at the battalion commissar, carrying a bottle of whiskey in his hand. "Have a taste of this!"

They had reviewed the volunteers of the XV Brigade, which was retreating from the Brunete front. It was a quiet day and there were no attacks. But George Nathan, who, ever since he set foot on the Peninsula, galloped wildly astride paradox after paradox, would leave this world with one final paradox. Through the mud of the Jarama, he had paraded his exquisite manners, he had led a group of Irishmen with whom in other times he would have clashed, he had ordered everyone to duck down while he stood straight up and volleyed jokes at the hundreds of rifles pointing back at him, and in a harsh world where men could not be attracted to other men, everyone had accepted that George Nathan loved men.

On the horizon appeared the silhouette of planes, and the commissar urged him to take cover. For once, against his legendary custom, he did the same as everyone else. And when the planes were directly overhead, George Nathan ran. Soon after, he lay on the ground with a fragment of shrapnel incrusted in his shoulder.

He realized that he wouldn't get away with this one. The commissar, who saw his glassy skin and papery lips, saw it, too. They placed him carefully upon a stretcher. As they carried him toward the ambulance, he asked the men who surrounded him to sing him songs of the International Brigades.

They say that before he died he uttered his last wish: he requested the presence of the secretary-general of the British Communist Party and asked him to accept him as a member of the party. We will never know why someone who is about to die makes a request that he won't see granted. But maybe, just maybe, far from home, the former English agent had found a family and a *raison d'être* and this was how he wanted to die.

# The Writer Who Didn't
# Want to Write

On the Guadalajara front, Ludwig Renn led the attacks of the XI Brigade with a pencil in his hand. Or at least that is what journalist Jean-Richard Bloch declared, perceiving in Ludwig Renn the well-defined outline of an intellectual committed to the times he has been called upon to live.

He had come into the world swaddled with aristocracy and a thirty-two letter name, Arnold Friedrich Vieth von Golssenau. He left home to fight in World War I and, on his return, Arnold Friedrich retained his name and little more. In 1920, as an officer in the Dresden police, he refused to open fire on the workers' demonstrations. He ripped up his uniform. He threw himself into literature. He embraced the most ironclad Communism. And on the first work he published, instead of engraving the thirty-two letters of his name, he simply wrote "Ludwig Renn."

In July 1937, writers from all over the world were to meet in Madrid to take part in the Second Congress of Intellectuals in Defense of Culture. Ludwig Renn opened the session at the campus of the Ciudad Universitaria. He had come in from the Brunete front and he was still wearing his commandant's uniform. The visual image that Jean-Richard Bloch had described burst into the auditorium.

He asked those in attendance to use their pens as a weapon against fascism. Not everyone had to put on the uniform he was wearing, because you could also combat fascism by weaving trenches with words. Nevertheless, he had long made his choice, and it was as fearsome as it was transparent. He was speaking for Maté Zalka, John Cookson, Ralph Fox, and Pablo de la Torriente. "We writers who are fighting at the front have left our pens behind because we don't want to write history, but to make history."

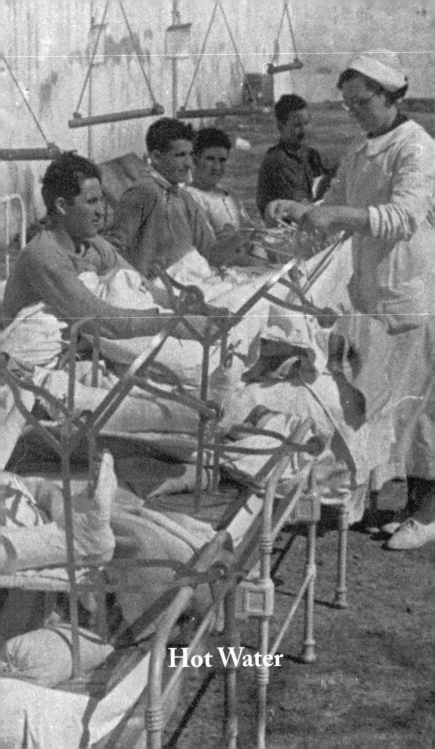

Hot Water

Some nurses were aware of the danger of fascism. They landed on the Peninsula with the professed intention of combatting it. Others who made the journey were driven by ethics or humanitarian reasons and in the war hospitals the work they did took on a political meaning they had not seen before.

And then there was Molly Murphy. She was a veteran—in more ways than one. During World War I, she had served in the Red Cross. She had visited the Soviet Union and she and her husband had met Lenin. She had abandoned the Communist Party and joined the Labour Party. And she had devoted her entire youth to fighting for the political and social rights of British women. She had participated in the suffragist movement, which demanded the vote for women and had shaken the foundations of British society.

In the 1930s, she watched in horror as the fascist movement led by Oswald Mosley spread through the streets of England. All of Europe was slipping toward darkness and at the height of that convulsion, in July of 1936, the fascist generals had risen up against the Republic. No one had to enlighten her as to what would happen to women if fascism continued devouring borders. When she reached the hospital she had been assigned to, at the Madrid front, she was twice the age of her fellow nurses and she had a fourteen-year-old son. Like them, she worked through day and night shifts until she collapsed from exhaustion.

In her letters home, she let her family know she was alive. She told them of the harshness of daily life in the hospital, and explained that since there weren't enough beds, she had to sleep in a cot cemented with dry blood. This is why, the day she turned forty-seven, her birthday gift from the doctors and nurses was hot water so she could wash her feet. In her letter, she put it this way, "They promised that for my next birthday I would get a little more, for the rest of my body."[10]

Beating the Odds

The ship drifted a mile and a half from the coast and, if Bill van Felix stretched out his arm, the outline of the coastal mountains could fit into his hand. A minute later, the waves sucked him down and the coast fled behind an abyss of water.

If the ship you are traveling on is struck by a torpedo and disappears beneath the waves and the freezing waters of the month of May, what are the odds of coming out alive?

Bill van Felix was twenty-one years old, he was from Brooklyn, and he had boarded the *Ciudad de Barcelona* in the port of Marseille, along with hundreds of young men who wanted to aid the Republic. Right around Cap de Creus, they had sighted an Italian submarine that pursued them like a shadow. Unable to shake their pursuer, on the Maresme coast the captain had made a desperate maneuver to get as close as possible to the beach. The submarine struck. The first torpedo went astray off the coast of Lloret. The second struck dead on in the machine room.

Bill van Felix had a feline gaze and was ferociously attractive— and would continue to be until he was an old man. Against all logic, he swam, determined to reach terra firma and beat the odds. That day, the fishing boats of the Maresme reeled in men instead of fish.

He got there in time to fight on the Ebre front, be wounded, flee from the hospital when the Francoists entered Catalonia, and run limping to the border.

If you survive all of this, it could be said that you have a debt with death.

During World War II, Bill van Felix enrolled in the U.S. Army. He went back to war, this time in the Pacific. He was on a ship. The ship was torpedoed.

When he died, an old man, death was sitting there, tired of waiting.

Mothers

In the San Francisco Marine Hospital, the patients discussed the course of the Spanish Civil War in front of a map they had hung on a wall. One day in May 1937 their best friend, the nurse who had helped them out and cooked for them when they went on strike, walked out on them to join the very same war they had imagined every day on the map. The day Esther Silverstein left, they put a roll of bills in her hand. It amounted to fifty dollars, everything they had been able to scrounge up among themselves. Just in case she changed her mind one day and wanted to come home. Her family was poor and she knew what every one of those bills meant for their owners. But in Paris, before she reached the Peninsula, she attended a demonstration in support of the Republic. When it was over, she approached the organizers, who were gathering funds for the Republic and gave them the fifty dollars from her sailors. She didn't intend to return. Once on the Peninsula, they asked her what hospital she wanted to go to and she answered, "Wherever there is more work to be done."

That was Brunete, one of the most deadly battles of the war, where she assisted the Catalan surgeon Moisès Broggi in the operating room. She didn't speak Catalan or Spanish, and he didn't speak English, but this was no obstacle to their doing thirty operations in twenty hours without a break. What she would never forget, though, were the mothers in Lleida. She was there one afternoon when the children had been dismissed from school and had run to the market to buy candy. No one noticed the bombers until they were right over their heads and opening their hatches. When they flew away the only thing left were the broken bodies of the children scattered through the Dantesque geography of what had been the market, the shrieks of the mothers crying out for their children, and Esther there in the midst of it all, compelled by an unseen force to remain in place right where she was. "I will never forget Lleida as long as I live," she would later say in a speech in California. "Children must be able to buy candy in the market on the square without bombs raining down upon their heads."[11]

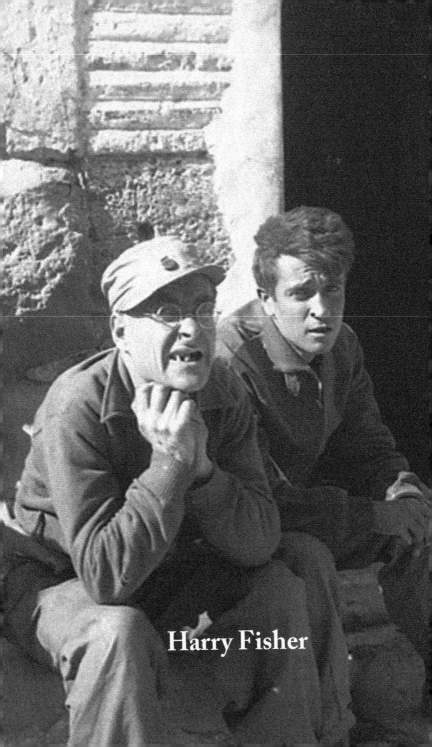

Harry Fisher

Harry Fisher condensed a number of lives into one single life. He was born in an orphanage for Jewish boys. He studied business, but lost his job when the Crash of '29 devastated the United States. He would wait outside a house where an eviction was going to take place, and as soon as the police left, leaving the family and their furniture in the street, he and a group of friends would break down the door and put all the furniture back so the family could move back in. He did anything to survive. He worked as a farmer, a bus driver, a merchant marine. None of it wiped away his smile and his gift for gathering stories.

During the Battle of Belchite, a strange thing happened. He was pinned down by a mortar shower and the only thing he could do was hug the ground like a cockroach. His eyes and throat were flooded with sand. The bombs went off just meters away from his flesh but, at some point, he stopped hearing them. His ears closed up. His muscles were made of stone. The world dissolved in the dust. His body was an empty box in which the shuddering of the earth resounded. It would be lifted a few centimeters and fall back to the ground, one shock after another. And then, he simply fell asleep.

But death did not find Harry Fisher sleeping. In March 2003, he was marching in New York in a demonstration against the invasion of Iraq. He was ninety-two years old. He fainted. A little while later, he was lying in a bed in St. Vincent's Hospital. He opened his eyes, asked where he was, and made one last observation: he had already been in that hospital, seventy years earlier, when they had sewn up the wounds that the police had inflicted on him during a strike. With this story on his lips, he died. He had been wounded by the police of his own country; he had participated in a war against Franco, Hitler, and Mussolini and had come out miraculously unscathed, untouched by a bullet or a scrap of shrapnel. Death came to him as he was fighting in the only place where he tended to get hurt.

Don't Close Your Eyes

Months after Harry Fisher fell asleep as the earth went into convulsions, another New Yorker, Alvah Bessie, lay under the sun of the Ebre River holding a rifle. His muscles were hard and his tongue was like cement, and when he swallowed saliva, he ingested earth. He realized he had fallen asleep when he saw that his hand was holding the stock of a weapon that no longer existed. A projectile or a piece of shrapnel had grazed his head and beheaded his rifle. The only thing left was the stock, which he was still gripping.

Bessie was a writer and a journalist who had traveled to the Peninsula for two reasons: to save his children from a world ruled by fascism and, also, because he felt that the comfortable life of a middle-class intellectual had numbed his limbs. He had become accustomed to opening the faucet and finding hot water and to lolling between the sheets until the sun was high in the sky. Now he felt a deep desire to find himself in a world without artifice, where humans would relinquish their personal privileges in the service of the common good.

He had only been at the Ebre for a couple of days when he understood that a soldier's existence fed on instincts that humanity had forgotten centuries before. That life is ruled by a daily struggle to be protected from cold, find food and water, and hold a cigarette in your fingers, perhaps in the inverse order. And that hugging the ground could mean clawing out one more day of life.

That day his body said one thing to him: if he tenses his muscles until they turned to stone, he could suddenly loosen up. Suddenly he felt the cold. He began moving his fingers as if he were playing an imaginary guitar and he drove his teeth into his dry lips. He blinked and blinked again, and ordered his eyes to jump from one stone to another, and he studied their shapes and colors and said to himself, "Think!" and he thought quickly, so quickly that the thoughts piled up on top of each other, because he had understood that if his eyes closed perhaps they would never open again, and if that happened, he would not know what had happened.

Ernst Busch

The German brigadistes greeted one man's arrival with an accordion. Many had seen him in the music halls of Frankfurt and Berlin, where he performed the works of Ernst Toller and Bertolt Brecht, before Hitler came into power. They had seen him perform in workers' theaters, they had heard his songs and turned them into hymns. Ernst Busch fled Germany with the Nazis in pursuit and took refuge all over Europe. Some time later, in the Thaelmann Brigade, it occurred to him to organize a chorale of one hundred voices. So that amid so much death and blood no one would forget one of the things that make us more human.

In March 1938, he shut himself up in the studios of Ràdio Barcelona to record a few of the songs they sang at the front. As fate would have it, those were the days when the Italian legionnaires' planes were releasing the worst of infernos upon the city. Three days of perpetual bombing, just intermittent enough so the people of Barcelona would think each attack was the last, but close enough so they couldn't shut their eyes to sleep. The sirens pierced the air, the planes arrived, and the people of Barcelona ran to the shelters or shut themselves up at home. Buildings collapsed, rescue patrols fanned out to aid the wounded, they cleaned up the rubble and the bodies as the planes took off and other Barcelonans picked up where they had left off, and suddenly the sirens announcing the next attack pierced the air again. For Mussolini, who had ordered the operation from an office in Rome, the whole city was the enemy, whether they were holding a rifle or a pacifier.

In the studios of Ràdio Barcelona, accompanied by a small chorus of German brigadistes, Ernst Busch let his voice pour forth. The recording would retain a murmur, subtle irregularities in the sound caused by the vibrations on the ground. They sang and the roof trembled. They sang as they did at the front, and that music has been saved forever more. Meanwhile, outside, the sky was falling and a thousand voices were being silenced.

Annie Murray

*I was on night duty for the first attack, so the war made a deep impression on me; because sick people are usually sicker at night, and at night our senses are sharply in tune with the gruesomeness and the awful suffering of the men, especially those with abdominal wounds and haemorrhage, for which one can do so little, became burnt into my brain. In those days many of the soldiers were under twenty years of age, and I shall never forget those young men with their torn bodies and their crushed limbs.* [12]

This was how Annie Murray described her first night in a hospital in Osca. She had grown up on a farm in Scotland, in a family of six sisters and two brothers, and she had studied nursing in Edinburgh. While she was working in the operating rooms, her two brothers were fighting on the front. Sometimes, when they had leave, her brothers would go see her at the hospital, but one day one of them showed up among the wounded. He survived, but he jumped out of bed and returned to the front too soon for her taste when he hadn't yet had enough time to recover.

She stayed in Barcelona until the fascist army was at the gates of the city. Her last patients were children who had lost their hands to the booby-trapped bombs that the planes threw out over Barcelona. She crossed the border with a deep, invisible wound that she would carry all her life. "The Spanish War had a terrific impact on me personally," she would explain. *It was the most important thing in my life. It was a tremendous experience that I would not have missed for any price. Naturally, I am not sorry to have gone. I came to know the struggles of the Spanish people and how joyful and generous they were with us. The people's spirit was incredible. I've never seen anything like it, and I don't think I ever will again.* [13]

Erika Glaser

The universal history of the twentieth century ran like a steam-roller over Erika Glaser. She was the daughter of a well-to-do German Jewish family with liberal beliefs. When Hitler came to power, they became fugitives. They took up residence in the Peninsula but before long history went looking for them. The first act of the great battle that would sweep across Europe was performed right before their eyes. They offered their services to the Republic. Willy Glaser had a medical degree from the University of Munich and he worked in hospitals in Castilla-La Mancha and Alacant. Therese Maria worked as a nurse. The couple's daughter did, too. Erika Glaser was fourteen years old. She must have been the youngest recruit in the International Brigades, but she worked as a physiotherapist in quite a few war hospitals.

They suffered the fate of the defeated. They followed a new path of exile to France. Willy was confined in one refugee camp, and the women in another. They were able to leave thanks to the help of foreign friends. Erika Glaser took up residence in Switzerland, in the home of a couple who offered shelter, protected from the conflagration of World War II. But history did not take a break. The curtain fell on that war and a new curtain rose on the Cold War.

Erika Glaser married a captain in the U.S. Army and had two children. They traveled to the German Democratic Republic to find out what had happened to her foster parents, who had disappeared in the whirlwind of Cold War intrigue. She was arrested and accused of having worked for the Office of Strategic Services of the United States, the seed of what would one day be the CIA. She survived the freezing winter of Siberia.

In stories of spies and double agents plots are woven like spider webs and narrative twists hide in blind spots. For some unknown reason, five years later, Moscow declared her innocent and released her. And Erika Glaser went back to the United States, was reunited with her family and resumed her life, or started a new one.

Frank Ryan

It couldn't have been easy to be a Marxist in a country where bishops made the rules and mayors obeyed them. Even so, the Irish still saw Frank Ryan as the hero of the independence movement, someone whose own life concerned him less than that of his people. He had been a commander in the IRA and he bore two wars on his back: the first, against the British; the second, against the Irish who had given their blessing to the partition of the country. He didn't need any more wars. But when Eoin O'Duffy, the head of the Irish fascists, announced that he would fight on Franco's side to save the Catholic faith, and priests, politicians, and journalists applauded his crusade, Frank Ryan slammed his fist down on the table so hard you could hear it in every county of Ireland. In December 1936, he sailed from the port of Dublin with eighty Irish antifascists. When he embarked, he left behind a country that condemned him to eternal hellfire.

He never returned. Mussolini's legionnaires captured him in Aragon. He refused to raise his arm in the fascist salute, as they obligated the prisoners to do. He informed his captors that he was a captain, even though this would cost him his life. He fought with the Francoist officers so that they would treat the prisoners like men and not animals. He gave them cause to shoot him twenty times over. And yet they didn't. The Gestapo took him to Germany. We don't know what happened to him. We know that the Nazis tried to convince him to lead an Irish uprising that would open a new war front, to weaken the British. And we know he died in Dresden, when he had been in prison for six years. Ireland had disavowed him for defending the Republic, but it cried out with one sole voice for the Nazis to free him. That is how important Frank Ryan was to the Irish. Michael O'Riordan would explain that his father was troubled when he took off to join the International Brigades, but he was even more troubled when he saw him come back alone. It is unforgivable, he would repeat, that you all came home and left Frank Ryan behind.

Merriman

A North American journalist who worked for the *Moscow News* was taken by surprise when he ran into Robert Merriman in a Paris bookstore carrying a pile of books about Spain in both hands. Not long before, they had been sharing tables at Moscow bars. But it couldn't be anyone else: twenty-seven years old, round glasses with thick frames, almost two meters tall, with the shoulders of a giant. Merriman declared that he intended to go to Spain to work on one of the collectivized farms. Since he was an economist, it could have been true, but as he was saying it, he averted his gaze. Soon both of them were leaving the bookstore and setting out to buy cartridge belts and gas masks, and a few days later they were on a train to the border, even though they had no idea how to go about joining the Republican ranks.

A few months later, Merriman told a journalist that that was no ordinary army. The soldiers were not simply soldiers. They were volunteers with a political consciousness and they demanded at least some small understanding of every action they were ordered to take. Their value as combatants did not reflect military experience, because few of them had any. They fought like lions because they knew why they were doing it. Nor was Merriman an ordinary commander. He didn't just shout an order and watch them carry it out. And when he was wounded, all he desired was to spend the least possible time between the clean sheets of the hospital.

In spring 1938, in the throes of the Francoist offensive, when Merriman had become the head of the General Staff of the XV Brigade, he and some of his men were surrounded near Gandesa. The last thing we know is that they tried to shoot their way out, unsuccessfully. On the other side of the Ebre, they waited for them for days. This photograph is all that's left. Perhaps it suggests the calm smile of a man who is exactly where he wants to be. Perhaps, too, the solitude of someone who has understood the weight of one's words when one is a captain.

The Legend

Milton Wolff was an art student from Brooklyn who never imagined he would one day be a soldier. He enlisted in the International Brigades and said to himself that he might soil his hands with the blood of the wounded while giving them first aid, but his fingers would never touch a weapon. The war would change his plans. The Battle of Teruel toppled his principles. In the middle of the battleground, with little time to think, he decided that his commitment to peace required him to grab a machine gun, aim at the fascists running toward him, and pull the trigger. Soon after, he would be the commandant of the Lincoln Battalion.

In April 1938, he would play the lead in an iconic scene. Without bullets. The Republicans had just lost the front of Aragon and had retreated to Catalonia, on the eastern shore of the Ebre River. The Lincoln survivors were scraping by in shacks made of branches on the riverbanks. They were accounting for missing friends who had died in flight or simply disappeared, swallowed up in the stampede. They were ghosts. They barely spoke. They cursed, they grumbled. Robert Merriman had been left behind. Milton Wolff, too. During the retreat, he had guided them with the grit of a veteran commander. But six days had gone by since they last saw him. And then this happened. A shout penetrated the litany of the valley. *El Llop! El Llop!* The Wolf, Milton Wolff, is back. The depressed men jumped to their feet and looked around. He was walking toward them, tall and taciturn. He shook everyone's hand and didn't stop to talk with anyone. He had escaped the siege of Franco's troops; Catalan farmers had taken him in and fed him. Then he had jumped into the Ebre River and swum across. He sat down in one of the shacks, asked for food, and started writing a letter to his girlfriend in Brooklyn. Outside, crowds were forming. That morning, the war had been lost, but suddenly it could be won again. This is what they all were thinking, and he knew it. He could tell that a myth was being woven around him, a legend that was too much for his twenty-two year-old self. This is why he kept his head down and wrote to his girlfriend in silence.

Jimmy Rutherford

"Your son was released on condition that he not go back to serve again in the Spanish War, and he broke his promise,"[14] said the Foreign Office in a letter to Jimmy Rutherford's father. "This is an offense that, under the ordinary laws of war, authorizes the side that has retaken a prisoner who had been freed on his word to punish him by death." It could be said that Jimmy Rutherford tempted fate and lost. But no one could tell him what he should do with his time, which was one of his few possessions.

The first time Franco's troops captured him was in the Battle of Jarama, and a military tribunal condemned him to death. They didn't shoot him because General Franco had decided to include him in a prisoner exchange. The son of Franco's ambassador in London wanted to interview the twenty-three British prisoners who would be freed. One by one. Then they took them to Irun where a photographer immortalized their final humiliation. The prisoners walked to the border flanked by hundreds of arms hailing them with the fascist salute. At the end of the gauntlet, the gate was lifted. They crossed the line and went back to the United Kingdom with one command: as long as the war lasted, they would not fight again alongside the Republicans.

Not long after, the brigadistes of the British Battalion saw the boy from Edinburgh, Jimmy Rutherford, arrive for the second time, happy and smiling. He was one of the few who had dared to challenge the norms and now he was exposing himself to the danger of dying in two different ways, in combat or by firing squad. And this was his fate. In March 1938, they captured him again. He changed his name to Jimmy Smalls and his mates tried to hide him. But the son of Franco's ambassador once again paid a visit to the prisoners. He wanted to see them one by one. And he never forgot a face.

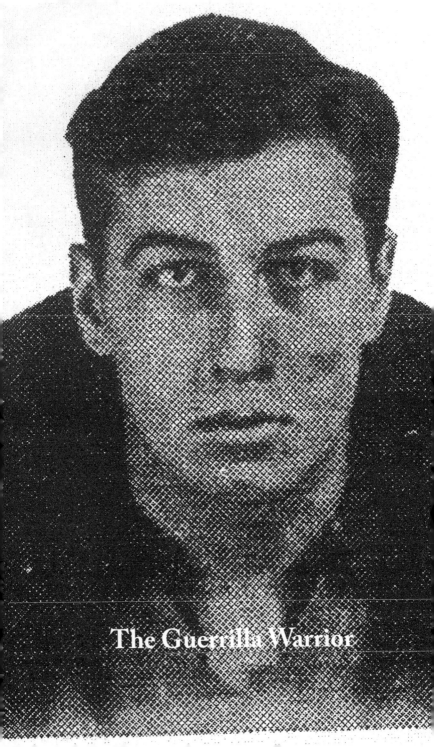

The Guerrilla Warrior

There are as many wars as persons who lived through them, and Bill Aalto's version relegates even the best adventure story to the category of a bland chronicle. By night, he would sneak into enemy territory. In the company of a handful of guerrilla warriors, he sent a train packed with Italian fascists flying into the air, he blew up the bridge at Teruel, he sabotaged Franco's lines of communication. His was a solitary nocturnal war, always walking a fragile tightrope, where every step he took brought him closer to an end far from his friends.

In May 1938, he led the boldest operation of the Republican guerrilla war. With his friend Irving Goff, at the head of a company of fifty volunteers, he sailed by night down the coast of Motril to cross into Francoist territory, assault a fort, and set three hundred Asturian prisoners free. But just as he was about to retreat behind Republican lines, an enemy patrol took him by surprise. Bill Aalto, Irving Goff, and two Spaniards were bringing up the rear and caught the eye of the Francoist troops. They ran until they were brought to a halt by a cliff that fell to the sea. They dropped their weapons and their clothing and jumped into the void. Aalto and Goff survived hidden between the rocks for three days and four nights. Stifled by cold, hunger, and thirst. Until, slipping into the water, they were finally able to return to the Republican lines.

Months later, when they were back in the United States, Bill Aalto assumed that the time had come to be bold again and tell his friend that he was gay. It was as if he had crossed the enemy lines once again, but this time with no one by his side. He was obligated to quit the Communist Party. He stopped attending the meetings of ex-brigadistes. He began to take refuge in alcohol. If he had fallen on the Peninsula, they would have honored him with a state funeral. But he was hunted down by cancer in an uncompromising United States and the hero of Motril died alone.

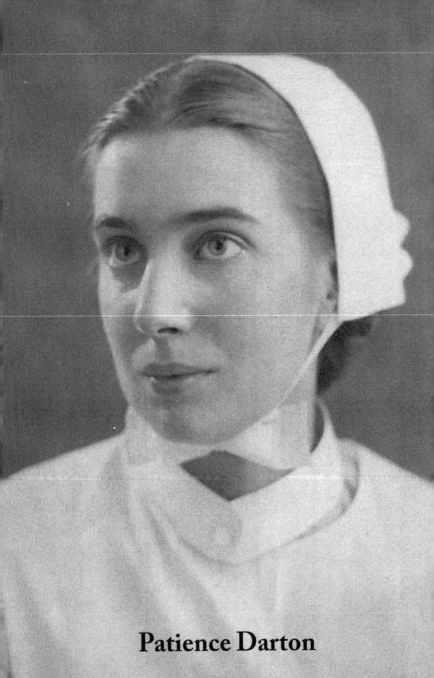

Patience Darton

Patience Darton was arguing with the Spanish commissar of a hospital, who was of the opinion that women shouldn't smoke because cigarettes were scarce and men were more entitled. When she couldn't get a fresh pack, she would scour the ground searching for butts. Seven butts equaled one cigarette. She was once described as a sort of angel, the nurse all the patients wanted by their side, but the person who said it had never seen her in a rage or gathering cigarette butts. Patience Darton kept the cap that nurses wore in England stored inside her suitcase. She considered it a ridiculous and useless artifact in the middle of a war. On the other hand, she would have been thankful for some trousers to make her life easier so she wouldn't have to run over to a bush and lift her skirt up to her waist several times a day.

Once the war was lost, she never mentioned that she had known a German brigadista by the name of Robert Aaquist. Nor did she mention the sorrow that invaded her as she deciphered the feelings that filtered through in his letters, nor their encounters and the obligation to be happy before parting once again, nor the fact that when he died it was she who wrote his parents. She didn't say a word until 1996, when she was eighty-five years old and she dared return to the Peninsula. She was to receive honorary Spanish citizenship with six hundred other brigadistes. But she didn't want to go back to the places where she and Robert Aaquist had been together. And a short time after she arrived in Madrid, she died.

"So we said a happy goodbye, and I climbed into the ambulance," she had written a short time after a fleeting meeting with him.[15] "Oddly, I kept looking out the window, not noticing anything and singing at the top of my lungs, wildly happy, without knowing why. In Spain, in general, I am happy, except when I am worried about the war, the international situation and the fascists, who seem to be very strong. Though it is wonderful to have a job from which to fight them… Well, that's a topic for another day. I was ridiculously happy, and I didn't know why…"

The Irishman

Sam Wild, the commanding officer of the British Battalion, ordered all the companies that crossed the Ebre River to carry a Republican flag and a Catalan flag on high. A symbolic gesture, perhaps, but in war symbols can move armies. And speaking of symbolic gestures, Sam Wild decided that one of the most appropriate candidates to carry the Catalan flag was a young Irishman who had fought in the ranks of the IRA.

And so it was that on the morning of July 25, 1938, in one of the barges carrying the British to the opposite shore of the Ebre, to the part of Catalonia occupied by the Francoists, Michael O'Riordan crossed the river with the Catalan flag in one hand.

He would never forget it. Nor would he forget what happened on the other shore.

On crossing the river, he handed the flag over to a Catalan soldier. And with this gesture he carried out what today we would see as a symbolic event: for months that land had lived beneath the boot of Franco's army, but now it was once again free and Catalan.

He didn't see the end of the battle. He was wounded on Hill 481, and his wound was serious enough for him to be withdrawn from the front.

In 2007, a little group of Irishmen appeared in Vinebre. They were carrying a funeral urn with the ashes of Michael O'Riordan. Their father and their grandfather. They scattered the ashes into the river current, at the exact spot from which O'Riordan had embarked that morning in 1938.

His son Manus sang a personal version of *La Santa Espina*. The Catalans who escorted them looked on in astonishment.

When he had been in Catalonia, during the Civil War, Michael O'Riordan had fallen in love with that traditional song. He sang it for years. A unique *Santa Espina* that may perhaps be sung to this day in an Irish house, in remembrance of a grandfather and the land he brought home with him.

René Cazala's Last Shot

René Cazala, an Algerian-born Frenchman, had a gift for achieving consensus among his superiors. They considered him a dyed-in-the-wool antifascist, and an accredited member of the Communist Party. And also an arrogant individual, who preferred personal glory to collective sacrifice, an unpredictable captain who was no fan of discipline and too much a fan of the anarchists. The perfect example of an officer no one wanted under his command.

But the night of July 24 to 25, 1938, the French crossed the Ebre River. They did it far from the larger theater of operations, skewing more toward the river delta. Their task was not to sneak in silence to the other side and slip like a dagger into Francoist territory. On the contrary, they were to draw the eyes and the bullets of the enemy to themselves and resist as long as they possibly could so that, to the north, thousands of Republicans could cross the river without interference and launch the great Ebre offensive. René Cazala had headed up one of the battalions ever since his old commander, Rabah Oussidhoum, a friend from Kabilia, had died. He led his men to the other shore, where they were not awaited by promises of glory. They were the only group who pulled it off. They found themselves caged in, with the fire of Franco's forces above their heads, a canal ahead of them, and the great tongue of water of the Ebre River behind them. Throughout an endless night, they clamored for aid, which never arrived, because the enemy fire made it impossible for anyone else to cross over. At dawn, the Paris Commune battalion, one of the most seasoned companies of the International Brigades, had ceased to exist.

With the first light, a few men were able to reach the place where a short time before the Paris Commune had fought. The cries no longer rang out and the riverbank was a long stretch of silence. They found René Cazala wounded. As they were carrying him off, the only thing he could think of was that all his fellow soldiers had died. He used his last bit of strength to take his pistol out of the holster and point it at his head. A shot rang out and his last bullet carried off all the words that might have been said.

**Valediction**

Back in the days when Pierre Landreux was selling *L'Humanité* in a Parisian square, the anarchists used to make fun of him. It's all well and good for you to ask for weapons for the Republic, they would say, but if you really want to help those people instead of preaching what you have to do is to go there and fight. Their mockery annoyed him but, little by little, without his giving it much thought, a seed was planted. A few months later, he showed up at an event featuring a young man from France who had been to the front. His name was Pierre Georges and he was seventeen years old. When he finished telling them the news from Spain, he asked who was ready to join the International Brigades. Pierre Landreux's arm shot up before his brain even ordered it.

One gesture can change a life. Landreux crossed the Pyrenees, went over the ridge, leaving peace behind, and walking into the war.

He was on the bank of the Ebre when, across the river, the boys from the Paris Commune Battalion were crying out in vain for reinforcements. Their cries, cut off by the explosions, pierced the night and lodged in Pierre Landreux's brain. With the first light, upriver, the battle wore on. The spectacle of that morning would haunt him forever. *The most terrible sight of that battle, which lives in my memory to this day, was to see amid the fog of dawn and the shore of the muddy, undulating waters of the Ebre, the bodies of our brothers-in-arms, fallen upriver when they were crossing the water. Still wearing their helmets or their caps, they flowed by endlessly. Still weighed down by their cartridges or grenades, that made them sink and rise to the surface, their heads or their torsos bobbed up from the water, as if they were floating dolls.*[16]

Wars engender images that defy comprehension. Only those who have experienced them have a right to turn them into words.

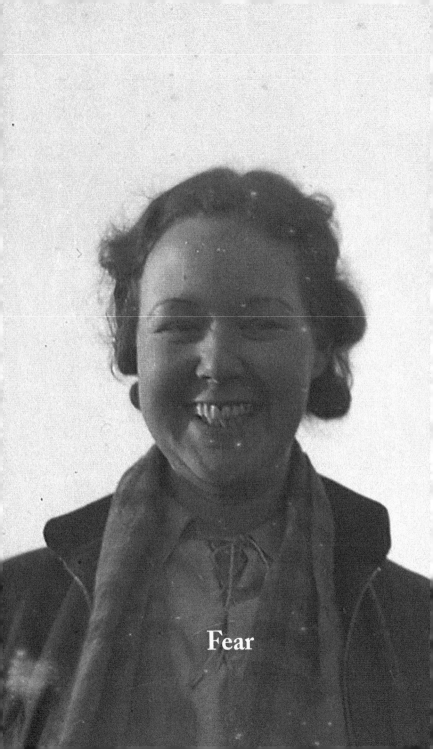

Fear

Maybe Lillian Urmston was destined to be a rebel, because her mother had Roma roots and her father claimed among his ancestors the illustrious Jack Cade who, five centuries before, had led a revolt against the King of England. But she learned her first real lesson far from her living room at home, when the crisis of the 1930s felled factories and filled the streets with unemployment and hunger.

During the Battle of the Ebre, Lillian Urmston served at the cave hospital at La Bisbal de Falset, far from the lines of fire where the soldiers had been wounded. She couldn't bear to be far from where she could be most useful, and she fought to be allowed to cross the river and set up a hospital at the Santa Magdalena hermitage, in the Serra de Cavalls. She worked there until the war crushed its walls. The medical staff took shelter in the train tunnels at Flix. Inside the tunnel, they attended to the wounded in the dark, operating by the light of oil lamps and cigarette lighters. When bombs fell on the mountain above them, she shivered.

But not out of fear. Fear was to fall alive into the hands of Franco's Moroccan soldiers. When they rushed a hospital, as a rule, they would kill every last wounded man. They tortured, mutilated, and raped the prisoners. During the retreat from Aragon, when the Republicans were stampeding in flight, battle lines disappeared and no one knew whether approaching vehicles belonged to enemies or friends. An unfamiliar chill engulfed her. She was only able to tell the tale because as it turned out the unmarked vehicles that approached them were always friends. Then the world returned to its original form: the beds, the wounded, the fellow nurses. Their skin was livid, and some were vomiting. Someone asked her, "Lillian, what's going on with your knees?"[17] And she realized they were shaking. Hours later, when the fear had dissipated, her knees continued to shake.

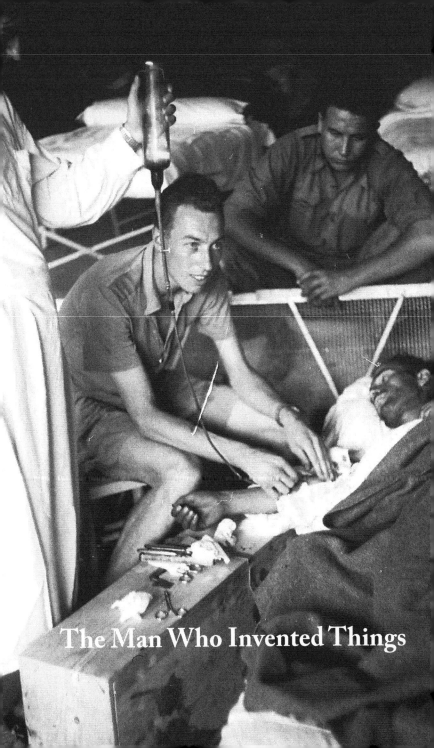

The Man Who Invented Things

His curriculum vitae was not promising. He was a doctor, but he didn't know how to amputate limbs or perform stomach operations. When he reached the first hospital, he found three surgeons and medical students who were acting as anesthetists. "And then there were the nurses, who found a solution for everything."[18]

Reginald Saxton was born in South Africa and had grown up in India and England, in upper-class Catholic boarding schools run with iron discipline. He had come out of there with no love of elites or talk of the All-Powerful, and instead of following the path that was expected of a young man of his class, he studied medicine, took an interest in economics, and embraced communism.

"You're going to be in charge of transfusions," they told him. And that decision, born of the need to give a job to a young man without a specialization, would end up saving thousands of lives. He pricked up his ears and absorbed everything he could learn. The problem was that in the Republican war hospitals there were no syringes or proper needles for the task they had charged him with. So he began to mull over how he could open the soldiers' veins to transfuse the blood, and he came up with a solution with the instruments he had at hand. He also created a method to handle the bottled blood that came to them from the rear guard. He found a way to install his transfusion apparatuses in mobile units that were taken directly to the front lines, where they were needed most. He showed his inventions to the other doctors and they came up with a system to supply and distribute blood that would be replicated all over Republican territory. And since the electricity supply to the hospitals was often cut off, he learned mechanics and invented a method to keep the reserves of blood cool.

He would never have said it himself, but someone else might well have said of him the same thing he said of the nurses: "And then there was Reggie Saxton, who found a solution for everything."

Nan Green's Blood

Nan Green gave a lot of thought to what boarding school she would send her children to. Instead of the most prestigious school in London, she chose a progressive institution, where she could be sure no one would punish them for the decision her parents had made.

As fate would have it, when she reached the Peninsula, they stationed her at the same hospital where her husband was working. It was a former convent in whose chapel she discovered all the preparations for a concert George Green had organized to lift the patients' spirits. He was a musician, and he would play the cello. A German patient with a leg wound would play the violin, even though he only knew how to play by ear. A Catalan patient, also wounded in the leg, would play the bandúrria, and the hospital plumber would play the guitar. An orphaned accordion waited for the hands that would pick it up. George Green showed Nan the instrument. "But I don't know how to play it!" she exclaimed. "By tonight you'll know,"[19] he answered. She had just enough time to learn a few chords and take part in an infernal spectacle performed for the patients.

Some time later, George Green asked to join the British Battalion to fight at the front as a soldier. Fate decided he was not to return. Fate, or the simple odds, determined that one in three of the brigadistes would remain forever in that land.

Nan Green worked as the secretary of the medical services all over the geography of the war, right down to the Ebre River. And, just as the nurses did, whenever the hospital needed blood, she would lend her arm. She would sit next to the wounded man and observe him. No matter who he was, his skin would be ashen and his lips gray. A thin tube tied their bodies together. Then the device would start sucking at her arm, one gulp after another. And as the blood flowed through the tube and disappeared into the man's body, the gray of his lips mutated into rosy tones. Years later she would say, "It was an experience I wouldn't have wanted to miss."[20]

FROM *Battlefields* OF SPAIN

TWO AMERICAN WOMEN

The Heroine

Ruth Davidow worked as a nurse in hospitals in Andalusia, Castile, Aragon, and the Ebre. When the fascists breached the Aragon defenses, she withdrew with the remains of the Republican army, setting up hospitals out in the open and watching as the bombs sent tents and wounded flying. She survived.

She was saved from the frying pan, but when she got back home, she learned that the fire awaited. The North American brigadistes had been labeled "premature antifascists" because they had committed the crime of combating fascism without the seal of approval of the government, when the White House had not yet taken an interest in fighting Hitler. Ruth Davidow responded drily to the accusation. "I am not a premature antifascist. I have been an antifascist all my life."

The years to come would confirm it. She defied the persecution of the government and the FBI, she was arrested, with the victory of the Cuban Revolution she set down in Havana, and in the late 1960s she volunteered to attend to the activists on the island of Alcatraz known as Indians of All Tribes, who occupied the former prison for eighteen months to defend the national rights of Native Americans.

But courage does not come all at once. In the midst of the Battle of the Ebre, when the Francoists repelled the Republican attack, she understood that the war could not be won. Ambulances overflowed. The hospital was bombarded. Every morning it seemed like a miracle that she was still alive. And one day she said enough. She hugged the doctors and nurses, said goodbye to the survivors, and went to the station without anyone's reproach. Who would have dared to criticize her for wanting to protect her life rather than immolate herself far from home for a lost cause? But this is what happened: the train she was to take stopped at the station and the stairs to the train car lay before her like a door to salvation. She couldn't move. She was simply incapable of boarding the train.

The Hill

The hill towered over the valley from a height of 666 meters above sea level, and no number is more precise than that of the devil. No one stayed there for more than ten days at a time. After ten days, survivors had to leave. The men who came to take their place saw a ghostly line file by, made up of silent men who looked without seeing, as if their souls had been ripped out. When their replacements reached the summit, they understood why. A lunar surface whipped by the wind awaited them—a nightmare of bare rock, where the last vestiges of life were the stumps of what one day had been bushes whose charred remains twisted among the stones. There were no trenches, nor were there human arms capable of digging them. The land was solid rock, impermeable to the entreaties of shovels and blades. It was a privileged lookout over the battles of the Ebre River, and hence it must be defended any way they could, even as artillery and airplanes emptied onto it all the lead that fit in the sky. The bombardments took place continuously, day and night, and there were no holes in which to hide. The hill was a grim metaphor of the struggles between machine and man, between lead and flesh.

One of the men atop the hill was Joe Bianca. An Italian-American with a Greek profile, an austere sailor, a veteran union member, a man with arms of solid steel, who would never ask of another what he could not do with his own hands. He had been honored with the stripes corresponding to the best soldiers in the Lincoln-Washington Battalion because during the last offensive of Franco's troops, when everyone was fleeing toward Catalonia as if pursued by the devil, he had continued to resist with a machine gun, keeping the fascists at bay so his mates could get away. It was hell to see how the bursts of a howitzer propelled his Herculean body upwards and how it traced a slow curve in the air as it fell, as if it were a rag doll. It was hell to see that as the airplanes approached, his brain ordered his legs to take off down the mountain, but they refused to get out of hell.

Hill 666

In the 1960s, a Catalan soldier who had fought by the side of brigadistes from Eastern Europe threw himself into writing the definitive history of the International Brigades. His name was Andreu Castells and he was a printer from Sabadell. He traveled all over Europe with his son to meet up with his former comrades-in-arms. He bought books in foreign bookstores and returned with a full backpack by clandestine routes through the Pyrenees. He would have the books written in English translated. In the summer, while his wife and son went swimming at the beach, he would be typing on a green Olivetti. He also launched an intense correspondence with former brigadistes.

In April 1975, he received a letter from Terry Maloney, a man from Sussex who had served in the XV Brigade. Summer after summer, for many years, he and his wife, Dorothy Toms, would load their suitcases into their car and drive to Andalusia. When they returned home, instead of driving directly north they would make a detour to the east and wend their way along the solitary roads at the foot of the Pàndols and Cavalls mountain ranges. They were no longer young, and the crossing had only the comforts that the narrow seats of a 1960s car could afford. Still, Terry Maloney could not resist following that route every summer. He would slow down and become very quiet. He would turn his head to see the mountain crest. The harsh profile of Hill 666 was outlined on the horizon, perfectly visible from the plains of Corbera d'Ebre and Gandesa. There it still stood, hard and intact. Dorothy Toms was also silent. She knew that those rocks were part of her husband's body, they lived inside of him just as they inhabited his nights. Terry Maloney corresponded with Andreu Castells in the Spanish he had learned as a soldier. In 1975 he wrote: *Since those days I have seen it many many times, because of our preference for going the long way when we travel to see Spanish friends in Jaén Province; naturally I cannot pass by it without taking a look; but I have never gone back up to the top. [...] it was impossible to bury our fallen comrades properly. I considered it a terrible place; uncomfortable, arid, without even a patch of shade; and very deadly.*[21]

The Last Man

When they were being bombed, the soldiers used to crawl into the holes dug by the mortar shells. Not just for protection from the shrapnel, but because the odds were better that another mortar would not fall where one had previously fallen. When the threat of death was imminent over a period of hours, obeying mathematics or superstition was the most reasonable of behaviors.

Alvah Bessie would remember a particularly frightened recruit he met at the Ebre, a boy obsessed with the notion that each instant was to be his last. He wasn't there of his own volition. He had been drafted when the Republican army had run out of volunteers and they had had to fill their ranks with both the children and the fathers of the rear guard. His tongue was coated with fear. He talked fast and he predicted that every day would be his last, almost as if he were calling for it. When Bessie learned a few days later that the boy had been taken down by a bullet, he was not surprised. At the front, those who most dreamed of death were the first to find it.

But there was one thing that filled them all, or almost all, with fear: dying the day of the last battle, when you knew that, if you managed to live to tomorrow, you would have averted all danger. In September 1938, the Republican Government announced that it would pull back all the international volunteers from the war front. On September 23, the International Brigades launched their last counterattack on the Ebre front. That day dozens of men died. But the last death would take a little longer. A photograph taken in early October on a street in Barcelona shows two great funeral wreaths. They were both for Chaskel Honigstein, a Pole from Lublin who had been wounded at the Ebre as he battled in the Jewish company known as Naftalí Botwin, and had died a few days later when the internationals were out of danger. They gave him a funeral service that was out of character in wartime. Those flowers summed up a fear they all shared.

A Glass of Wine Before Dying

Hans Landauer was seventeen when he reached the Peninsula and he left just before he turned eighteen, when there wasn't so much as a foot of Republican land left in Catalonia. He was so quick and agile that they called him the Rabbit and, when communications broke down, they would send him running from one trench to another with messages. Agustí Centelles, the photographer, took a picture of him on October 28, 1938, during the farewell ceremony the people of Barcelona dedicated to the International Brigades. In the photo, you see a boy with a bouquet of flowers in one hand directing a boyish smile to the camera. His feet rest on a carpet of petals and on either side you can sense thousands of voices bidding them all goodbye.

For him, though, the war didn't end that day. He was Austrian and could not return home because the fascists were in power. He stayed in Catalonia down to the last gasp and took part in the last battles, holding back the Francoist forces from La Garriga to the Pyrenees, to protect the population who were fleeing to France. He crossed the border a short time before the gendarmes closed the crossing. In France, he was awaited by three concentration camps and a prison. And in Germany, four years of confinement in the Nazi inferno of Dachau.

He would survive through more battles than most of us will ever see. But he lived to be an old man and one day he expressed a wish out loud. Before he died, he wanted to drink a glass of wine from the land where he had fought as a boy. To fill his body with those grapes before it shut down forever.

Stretching before many of those who fought in the International Brigades were lives teeming with history. They fought in the Resistance, or with the partisans, or in an army in World War II, or in Soviet or American prisons, and they reached the end of life with a catalogue of unspeakable struggles. But when they were old and on their deathbeds, the places many of them returned to were the Jarama and the Ebre. Perhaps because, as the Frenchman George Sossenko put it, that was where they lost their virginity.

Braina Voss

Braina Rudina Pedanova was born to a poor Jewish family in Riga, the capital of Latvia, and she would have lived an equally impoverished life if she had not been stubborn enough to contradict the fate that had been written for her. At the age of twenty, she took up residence in Germany to study medicine, and she joined the Communist Party. She spoke Latvian, German, Russian, French, Spanish, and Serbo-Croatian fluently. She lived in Germany until Hitler came into power and being Jewish and a Communist she was obliged to flee.

When the Civil War broke out, her husband and her sister set out for the Iberian Peninsula to join the Republic, and she went to Belgrade to organize the recruitment of Yugoslavian volunteers. The Government discovered her activities and arrested her. When she got out of prison, eight months later, she could have considered her aspirations to solidarity to have been satisfied, but instead she decided to embark on the same journey her husband and sister had made. She arrived in February 1938, in a dramatic moment: the Aragon front had been breached, the Republican army was fleeing east, and it wouldn't be long before the loyalist territory was broken in two. Braina Voss, for this was how she was known in the Civil War, became the director of the hospital at S'Agaró, on the Costa Brava, very close to the border. The medical staff included personnel from some twenty countries, and took in the sick and wounded who were to be evacuated to France.

She had arrived on the Peninsula in a dramatic moment and when she left a year later, the situation was worse. She crossed the border at Portbou with the last heartbeats of Republican Catalonia, amid long lines of refugees. With her was a North American nurse who had refused to leave with her compatriots and had wanted to stay to the end. In France, concentration camps awaited some of the doctors and nurses who came with her. What awaited her was Moscow, the Soviet medical services, and an old war with a new name.

Courage

While Gert Hoffmann was doing time in an Austrian prison for belonging to the Communist Youth, he received a gift from his father: it was a Spanish language book. His father had a feeling that when his son was set free he would set off to fight the fascists, and that is what he did.

But, in January 1939, he was experiencing a situation he had not foreseen. He had fought at the Ebre but it had been three months since he last touched a weapon. Since the retreat of the internationals had been decreed, the Austrians were watching time tick by in La Bisbal d'Empordà. They couldn't go home because Austria was now under the Third Reich. And the French government, which feared they would turn into refugees, stateless people in the land of enlightenment, had closed the border to them. Germans, Italians, Latin Americans, and Eastern Europeans had all come to the same dead end. They couldn't move. All they could do was listen to the news—which wasn't good. Franco had burst through the Ebre and Segre defenses, he was invading Catalonia, and galloping north.

In late January the Republican authorities made a desperate move: they begged the stranded international soldiers to return to the front to help the last defense forces and protect the civilian population who were fleeing to France. To return to the front, with no weapons, when all hope was lost. The Austrians heard their plea, and many years later Gert Hoffman would tell this story to journalist Eloi Vila:[22] *Men who believed themselves to be no longer in danger from the risks of the war suddenly found themselves facing it again. Men who had escaped with their lives from so many dangers would run the risk of losing those lives at the last moment, sacrificing them, at that, without the illusion of victory, but rather just to protect a retreat that would end in exile. Even so, very few of them refused the call, but among those who did was a short, thin man. When the meeting was over his mates asked why he hadn't enlisted. His response was simple: "Because I'm a coward." I was impressed by his courage. I would not have been so brave.*

Write My Name

When he wrote down the 684th name, Jose Gay da Cunha was finishing up one of the most painful jobs he had ever done. It had been three months since they last fought, there weren't enough weapons for all of them, and he knew that each of those men was on a path to suicide. The last name he wrote belonged to Valdés, the Cuban. When he heard that they had promoted him to sergeant, Valdés was moved to tears.

Gay da Cunha went back to the office of the General Staff in Cassà de la Selva. He had participated in an insurrection in Brazil, he had lived through exile, and he had been fighting Franco for about a year. He had seen everything. But he was not prepared to confront the rage of Román López Silveira, who was waiting for him in the office. Silveira was Uruguayan and he was sick. And he was furious because he had not been included on the list. Gay da Cunha wanted to explain. It was clear the state of his health did not allow him to join an expedition like that, in which he would have to fight without a break for days or weeks. Román wouldn't listen; he had come to combat the fascists and, if they didn't assign him, he would desert and join the first group of Republicans he came across to fight with them. Gay da Cunha tried to reason with him but, convinced that he would follow through on his threat, he gave in and added his name to the list.

At that point, Regino Baes, another Uruguayan, showed up. He seemed just as furious as Román had been a short while before. He was too old for that mission, Gay da Cunha told him. His words also fell on deaf ears. He wanted to defend every foot of land of Republican Catalonia, he told the man, and he didn't care what the commandant thought. And that was how one more name was added to the list of the last Latin American volunteers.

There is an epic in defeat that victory cannot equal. We can say that now. But when the train transported those men toward the south, Jose Gay da Cunha saw only 686 comrades that he would never see again. That train, he would write, carried off a very large piece of the heart of the XV Brigade.

The Landless

Ave Bruzzichesi was Catholic and had nothing to do with politics. Until one spring day in 1937, in the New York Hippodrome Theatre, when she heard the Irish chaplain, Michael O'Flanagan, make an appeal to doctors and nurses who loved their profession to go to the Peninsula to help the Republic. She had worked on the war fronts, and when the Republican government ordered the retreat of the Internationals, she disobeyed the order. Like many nurses and doctors who love their professions, she refused to abandon the wounded in their hospital beds.

"Barcelona was dying in the last days of January 1939 and to watch a city die is just as horrible as watching a person die,"[23] Juan Miguel de Mora would write. Ave Bruzzichesi was there, as the air raids devastated the city. Along with the lead the planes unloaded, they were dropping packages labeled "Chocolate," which the children ran to pick up. There were bombs inside. The last patients she attended to in Barcelona were children with no hands.

She left as Franco's troops were entering, and she joined the exodus to the border. She saw the gendarmes treat the Republicans like prisoners-of-war and confine them in barbed wire spaces, without baths or coats or medicine. She stayed two months, caring for them with whatever she had, which was little more than her hands.

And she went home. She never tired of condemning the fascists and the French government. Every time she got near a microphone, she would evoke the thousands of men, women, and children who were forced to live like animals. She also recalled the others who loved their professions: the Austrian surgeons, the Hungarian nurses with whom she had shared operating rooms, who had no home because fascism was in power in the countries they came from, the landless people of her time, pursued by the Nazis, who were no longer anywhere because the sand and sewers of the French camps had carried them off.

Paula Draxler

The photographs of Paula Draxler show an almost girlish smile. Like those of many nurses and soldiers, captured on the camera in the scarce moments they were neither working nor at the front, contradicting the serious grimaces we take for granted in war photography.

She was a secretary in the Military Intelligence Service, and she did nursing duty in hospitals in Vic, Murcia, and Mataró. But Braina Voss didn't like her. She considered her little inclined to discipline and more concerned with spending time with friends than with working at the frantic rhythm the hospitals required. We should never look at anyone through another's eyes. A report written in March 1940, when the Civil War was already lost, profiled a Paula Draxler whom Braina Voss would not have recognized: a young woman with scant political preparation, and a secretary and nurse committed to fulfilling her duties.

We will never know how much truth there was in the report, nor what she thought of it all. We will also never know if one day the war was just too much for her. She had arrived from Austria in February 1937, and she couldn't go home. In 1939, when Franco's troops occupied Catalonia, she crossed the border with the long columns of refugees and with the brigadistes who no longer had a home. She managed to escape from the internment camps and join the French Resistance. She lived a new life in the shadows and continued to fight the Nazis. Until 1944. That year, with the final throes of the German occupation, she died.

Nothing is certain about Paula Draxler, not even the end. Two stories have been written of her last day. It matters little whether the Gestapo captured and shot her or if, on finding herself trapped, she decided to jump out the window.

Frida Stewart

The doors of the concentration camps in Gurs were open to those who had no place to go home to. There the French government confined thousands of brigadistes who couldn't return to their countries of origin and a few, not many, who were waiting for their passports. Crowded in there were Germans, Poles, Italians, and volunteers of other nationalities, waiting for the escape networks of the French Communist Party to help them flee.

Frida Stewart left behind the comfort of England to help the prisoners of Gurs and other camps. It was not the first time she had done it. Before the war broke out, she had studied music and dramatic arts and had directed theatrical projects for unemployed English workers. She was neither a doctor nor a nurse nor an X-ray technician, but she had climbed onto an ambulance, traveled to the border, and entered the Peninsula as a driver. She worked in a hospital for refugee children in Murcia and wrote articles in English to combat the blockade her government had imposed on the Republic. At the end of the war she helped in the camps for Basque refugee children, organized musical events to raise funds, and visited the French camps. Not long after, Hitler invaded Poland and the curtain was raised on World War II. Frida Stewart, who hadn't budged from France, was arrested by the Gestapo. She was a prisoner of the Nazis for a year, until she was able to escape with the aid of the French Resistance.

She ended the story as she had begun it. In 1936, when she was twenty-six years old, not long before she climbed onto that ambulance, she had organized committees in Hull and York to aid the Republic and bring down the blockade. In 1992, when she was a grandmother, she left the comfort of England once again, traveled to Cuba, observed the toll that isolation and the blockade were causing there and, on her return to Cambridge, at eighty-two years of age, she did the same thing she had done in 1936.

Roberto Vincenzi

The Italians in the Garibaldi Battalion could take pride in having crushed Mussolini's fascists in the Battle of Guadalajara. But when a white coat approached, their proverbial courage went up in smoke. One rainy night Penny Phelps, a British nurse, showed up in Quintanar de la República, where the volunteers of the Garibaldi Battalion had been ravaged by an epidemic of scarlet fever and typhus. She imposed order on the chaos and when she had all the soldiers vaccinated and showered, she showed up in the officers' mess with a tray full of syringes and made them lock the door. When the officers saw the content of the tray they burst into riotous laughter. When they understood that she intended to jab them one by one and inject a strange liquid into their veins, panic flooded the room. To no avail.

During the weeks Penny Phelps worked in that town, she met a young officer, Roberto Vincenzi. He was intent on teaching her Castilian, they fell in love, and ended up getting engaged. The paths of war separated them but, in 1939, Penny Phelps combed the French concentration camps until she found him. She sent him cigarettes and wrote him letters. She told him that she had fallen in love with another man, the doctor who had cured the wounds she suffered in the war, and she had married him.

"I was afraid the wounds that plane inflicted on you had taken your life. Penny, you married, you did the right thing. How could I blame you? In my situation, how could I fulfill my promise? I am surrounded by barbed wire," he responded. "In your letter you ask me not to feel bitterly toward your husband. What fault is it of his? How could I condemn a man who must be giving you the happiness I cannot give you."[24] A short time after Roberto Vincenzi wrote that letter, the German army occupied France. And then, as happened with so many other prisoners, the earth swallowed him up.

Where is My Home?

We ask ourselves how someone can leave behind home, family, work, even peace, to go to a distant country where a war is raging. And not just to see the war, but to live it. And we forget an essential question: how does one go back, from a world at war to a world in peace? When we make this journey, what pieces of ourselves do we lose along the way?

Penny Phelps was wounded by a mortar strike as she tended to soldiers in a hospital in Castelló. She woke up covered in bandages. A doctor came over to her and said that she had been one of the lucky ones. They evacuated her to London and, there, bit by bit, she regained consciousness. The first days she thought it had all been a dream, or someone else's life. Sometimes she believed that the dream was the world of white hospital walls and English sun filtering through the window. As if she could not reconcile within one same being two such conflicting realities. She thought about George Nathan, whose hand she had held as he lay dying in Brunete, and she wondered if he was still alive. When she walked down the streets of her city, if she heard the sound of an engine in the sky she ran to take cover in the first doorway she could find. Quite some time would go by before she realized that everyone was looking at her and that bombs would not rain down.

Juan Miguel de Mora was from Mexico and he fought at the Ebre at the age of sixteen. He spent one endless week on Hill 666. Where the bombs dropped from the naked sky onto stone and men. He went back to Mexico with an intact body but a fractured soul. He couldn't make his friends or family understand the shattering in his gut. In a world where everything was just as he had left it and nothing had been broken. How could a fellow Mexican understand that on that hill the worst thing was not the bombings but the minutes of silence that preceded them? How could he explain that void to someone who hadn't experienced it? He had fought at the Ebre, yes. But for many years he was incapable of remembering it. The veil that shrouded the days on the Ebre only lifted when he was seventy-nine years old.

Aileen

In 1939, a young woman threw red paint on the door of the headquarters of the British government, at 10 Downing Street in London. It was a gesture of protest against Chamberlain's non-intervention policy, which had left the Republic unaided and with its hands tied in the face of the tanks and planes of Franco, Hitler, and Mussolini. Her name was Aileen Palmer and she was from Australia. She was a translator and a poet, and she wore her hair short like a boy.

In July 1936, she was in Barcelona with her parents, working on the organization of the People's Olympiad, when the fascists rebelled against the Republic. She saw how the people of Barcelona rose up against the military and crushed them in the streets. The outbreak of the war forced the Palmers to flee to England, but soon Aileen decided that she wanted to return. She broke off her family ties, and since she spoke Spanish, French, Russian, and German fluently, she worked as a translator in a medical unit of the International Brigades. On the front lines, the fruits of Chamberlain's policy pummeled her over and over. Every time an ambulance drove up to the hospital and unloaded dozens of bodies broken by the Italian and German bombs.

The clamor of the war pursued her all her life. When she returned to Australia, she realized she didn't have a home. Her parents, two prestigious writers, would never approve of her wanting to be a poet and not behaving as was expected of a young woman. Poems of shame, short hair, flashes of shattered bodies, unrealized desires, and mental illness. None of this could be cured by her parents, or by the laws of society, or the beds in psychiatric wards, or the electroshock therapies of the Australian institutions. All they did was to turn her memory into a shattered mosaic. Through which the sound of war filtered in on thin wires.

Colonel Fabien

In Paris, there is a Place du Colonel Fabien and a metro stop with this same nom de guerre. Behind it is hidden Pierre Georges, the third of four brothers of a family of union men. His father didn't want him to go to the Peninsula, because he was only sixteen years old, but he falsified the age on his passport and, in October 1936, he showed up in the encampment of the International Brigades. He came to be an officer of the La Marseillaise Brigade and, two years later, he returned home with scars from lead slugs in his thigh, his arm, and his belly. But this is not why he is still remembered today with a square and a metro station in Paris.

Two years after that, Pierre Georges was married. The birth of his daughter, Monique, had been a window of joy in a bleak time. The German army circulated through the streets of Paris. People disappeared every night, but during the day, the soldiers were courteous with the passersby, like polite guests in the house of their hosts. The Parisians lowered their heads, fearful and ashamed. Paris was a gray canvas and a sad conspiracy of silences. The Resistance, still timid, printed out clandestine pamphlets against the occupation, and hid those who were on the run, but, in France, only German hands bore arms. One day, Henri Tanguy, a former commandant at the Ebre, went looking for Pierre Georges. For him and for a few more who had fought on the Peninsula. Everything had to change.

On August 21, 1941, Pierre Georges strode through the crowd that circulated on the Barbès metro platform. His hand was in his pocket. An officer of the German marine corps contemplated the choreography of the movements traced by the Parisians. Georges approached him. He grasped the handle of a small 6.35 caliber pistol. If the German met his eyes, he saw that the gaze of the man before him was not like that of the other Parisians. But it would be too late. In that instant, both the German officer and the entire Barbès station heard the sound of the first bullet of the French Resistance.

Rol-Tanguy

The last German governor of Paris appears in a photograph atop a tank, flanked by French soldiers. He has just surrendered. The city, as Jean-Paul Sartre would write, has gone through an apocalyptic week, but it is finally free again. Close by the general is the commandant of the French Forces of the Interior, the man who directed the guerrilla insurgency that has blocked off the Parisian sewers and turned the city into a mousetrap for the Germans. He calls himself Rol, but until now, his name had been another, Henri Tanguy, and he is wearing his old uniform from the International Brigades.

Some years back, when the fascists rose up against the Republic, he was a young metalworker from the Paris region and one of the most promising leaders of the French Communist Party. In February 1937, he appeared in Austerlitz Station with other party leaders and boarded a train that took him to the south of the Pyrenees. He commanded two battalions, he was the political commissar of the Marseillaise Brigade, and he returned to France with a bullet incrusted in his shoulder blade. He also returned with a hole inside him, opened by the Battle of the Ebre, which carried off a friend of his. His friend's name was Rol, Théophile Rol.

Later he would lead the Resistance. He recruited former brigadistes for the insurrection. He wanted his nom de guerre to be Rol. He dressed once again, as he had at the Ebre. He appeared in the photograph.

For a long time, the French were unaware that Henri Tanguy's war had begin south of the Pyrenees in 1936, long before the Nazis filled France with fear. But he knew from the first day. This is why, after the week of the apocalypse, he changed his last name, and he grew old and died as Henri Rol-Tanguy, half himself, half his friend, half France and half Ebre. And he passed the name on to his children, so that the place where this story began should always be remembered.

# NOTES

1. Yvonne Scholten, "Fanny, Queen of the Machine Gun," *The Volunteer*, December 4, 2011. Yvonne Scholten is also the author of Fanny Schoonheyt's biography.

2. James Yates, *Mississippi to Madrid: Memoir of a Black American in the Lincoln Brigade* (Greensboro, NC: Open Hand Pub., 1989).

3. Rémi Skoutelsky, *Novedad en el frente: Las Brigadas Internacionales en la Guerra Civil* (Madrid: Temas de Hoy, 2006), 101.

4. Pablo de la Torriente Brau, *Peleando con los milicianos* (La Habana: Editora Política, 1987), 22.

5. Peter N. Carroll, *The Odyssey of the Abraham Lincoln Brigade: Americans in the Spanish Civil War* (Stanford, CA: Stanford University Press, 1994).

6. Nancy Phillips, Georgia Weber, and Lise Vogel, "Las mujeres americanas y la Guerra Civil española," Asociación de Amigos de las Brigadas Internacionales. www.brigadasinternacionales.org.

7. Paul Preston, "Two Doctors and One Cause: Len Crome and Reginald Saxton in the International Brigades", *International Journal of Iberian Studies* 19(1) (2006): 5–24.

8. Ibid.

9. Mika Etchebéhère, *Mi guerra de España: Testimonio de una miliciana al mando de una columna del POUM* (Barcelona: Alikornio, 2003), 53–54.

10. Angela Jackson, *British Women and the Spanish Civil War* (London: Routledge, 2002).

11. Frances Patai, "Mujeres voluntarias estadounidenses en la Guerra Civil española: humanitarias, antifascistas, activistas para la vida," ALBA. Frances Patai Papers. ALBA 131. Series II: Writings. Box 5, Folder 15. [Article originally in Spanish].

12. Annie Murray, "I Shall Never Forget," in Jim Fyrth and Sally Alexander (eds.), *Women's Voices from the Spanish Civil War* (London: Lawrence and Wishart, 1991), 61. [This is a direct quote translated from the original Catalan].

13. Ian MacDougall (ed.), *Voices from the Spanish Civil War: Personal Recollections of Scottish Volunteers in Republican Spain 1936–39* (Edinburgh: Polygon, 1986), 74.

14. Letter from the Foreign Office to James Rutherford, IBMA. Box 28/H/4. [Carta del Foreign Office a James Rutherford. IBMA. Box 28/H/4].

15. Angela Jackson, *"For us it was Heaven.' The Passion, Grief and Fortitude of Patience Darton: From the Spanish Civil War to Mao's China"* (Brighton: Sussex Academic Press, 2012). We owe much of what we know of Patience Darton to historian Angela Jackson and in particular to this book. (JM-R). [Angela Jackson, *Para nosotras era el cielo: Pasión, dolor y fortaleza de Patience Darton: De la Guerra Civil española a la China de Mao* (Barcelona: Ediciones San Juan de Dios, Campus Docent, 2012)].

16. Robert Coale, "Las Brigadas Internacionales en la Batalla del Ebro," in Josep Sánchez Cervelló and Sebastián J. Agudo Blanco (eds.), *Congreso Internacional sobre la Batalla del Ebro: Ponencias: Vol. I* (Tarragona: Arola, 2011), 246–247.

17. Angela Jackson, *British Women and the Spanish Civil War* (London: Routledge/Canada Blanch Studies on Contemporary Spain, 2002).

18. Paul Preston, "Two Doctors and One Cause: Len Crome and Reginald Saxton in the International Brigades," *International Journal of Iberian Studies* 19(1).

19. Nan Green, "Small Beer," in Jim Fyrth and Sally Alexander (eds.), *Women's Voices from the Spanish Civil War* (London: Lawrence & Wishart, 1991), 88.

20. Angela Jackson, *British Women and the Spanish Civil War* (London: Routledge/Canada Blanch Studies on Contemporary Spain, 2002), 29.

21. Letter from Terry Maloney to Andreu Castells (April 21, 1975), Arxiu Històric de Sabadell, Andreu Castells Papers. [Carta de Terry Maloney a Andreu Castells (April 21. 1975), Arxiu Històric de Sabadell, Fons Andreu Castells].

22. Eloi Vila (ed.), *Cartes des del front* (Barcelona: Ara Llibres, 2012), 98.

23. Juan Miguel de Mora, *La libertad, Sancho ...: Memorias de un soldado de las Brigadas Internacionales* (Cuenca: Ediciones de la Universidad de Castilla-La Mancha, Libros para Todos, 2008).

24. Letter from Roberto Vincenzi to Penny Phelps (Gurs, July 1, 1939), reproduced in Angela Jackson, *British Women and the Spanish Civil War*.

# Sources

## Unpublished Sources

"A Negro Nurse in Republican Spain." Issued by The Negro Committee to Aid Spain with the Medical Bureau and North American Committee to Aid Spanish Democracy. New York. Universitat de Barcelona. Library of the Republican Pavilion.

"A typed biography about Salaria Kea entrance into the medical field and her experience in Spain." ALBA. Frances Patai Papers. ALBA 131. Series I: Biographical Files. Title: Kea, Salaria (O'Reilly). Box 2, Folder 12. ["While Passing Through," unpublished autobiographical account by Salaria Kea].

Albrighton, James. "Diaries." IBMA. Box 50. File Al/12.

Anon. "Statement made re Frank Ryan—International Brigader by American Comrade—Prisoner with Ryan in Spain." IBMA [International Brigade Memorial Archive. Marx Memorial Library. London]. Box 28, Prisoners of War. File G: Material on Frank Ryan. Doc. G/3.

Bates, W[inifred]. "In Teruel with the British and American Medical Services. Front of Teruel, January 1938." IBMA. Box 29. File D. Doc. D/17.

Dingle, B. "Blood transfusion in Spain." IBMA. Box 29. File D. Doc. D/I.

"Excerpts from 'While Passing Through'." IBMA. Box D-2, American Nurses & Medical Staff; Reporters & Supporters. File D: Salaria Kea (O'Reilly)—nurse. Doc. D/I

Foreign Office. Letter to James Rutherford. IBMA. Box 28/H/4.

Foss, James. *William Aalto: A Hero of the Left.* ALBA. Abraham Lincoln Brigade Archives Vertical Files / Series I: ALBA Individual Files. "Aalto, William: James Foss Manuscript."

"Frank Ryan. Support Demand for his Release from Franco Prison." IBMA. Box H-12. Ry/2.

"Frank Ryan's Fate—Dublin Plea to Secure his Release." IBMA. Box A-12. Ry/I.

Gerassi, John. "Interview with Irving Goff." ALBA. John Gerassi Papers. ALBA 018. Series I: Oral History Transcripts. Box 3, Folder 3. Los Angeles, August 24, 1980.

Harriman, Manny. "Interview with Irving Goff in Which He Discusses William (Bill) Aalto and other Veterans." ALBA. Col. Manny

Harriman Video, Oral History Collection. ALBA V 48-001. [No date].

Hutchins, Evelyn. "Albert Prago Papers. Contribution to *Our Fight*." ALBA 135. Box 2. Folder 7.

Hutchins, Evelyn. "John Dollard Research Files for Fear and Courage under Battle Conditions." ALBA 122. Box I. Folder 21.

Hutchins, Evelyn. "The Good Fight." ALBA 210. Box I. Folder 50.

Jones, Tom. "Major Frank Ryan. Adjutant of the 15th International Brigade of the Spanish Republican Army Captured by Spanish Fascists in 1938—Sentenced to Death. Died in Germany. Irish Patriot and Socialist." IBMA. Box 28, G/13. [February 1975].

[Kea O'Reilly, Salaria]. "A set of questions that she answered for the Biographical Statistics of the American Medical Bureau and Co Workers." ALBA. Frances Patai Papers. ALBA 131. Series I: Biographical Files. Title: Kea, Salaria (O'Reilly). Box 2, Folder 12.

[Kea O'Reilly, Salaria]. "A Typed Biographical Background by Salaria Kea Describing Her Life Growing Up and the Racism That She Experienced." ALBA. Frances Patai Papers. ALBA 131. Series I: Biographical Files. Title: Kea, Salaria (O'Reilly). Box 2, Folder 12.

[Kea O'Reilly, Salaria]. "May Every Knock Be a Boost." ALBA. Frances Patai Papers. ALBA 131. Series I: Biographical Files. Title: Kea, Salaria (O'Reilly). Box 2, Folder 12.

Lossowski, Vincent. "A Letter by 12/6/1938, that Describes the Liberation of 300 Asturian Prisoners in a Guerrilla Attack Led by Captain William Aalto." ALBA [Abraham Lincoln Brigade Archives. Tamiment Library. New York University. New York]. Vincent Lossowski Papers. ALBA 071. Series I, Correspondence.

Maloney, Terry. Letter to Andreu Castells (April 21, 1975). Arxiu Històric de Sabadell [Sabadell Historical Archive]. Andreu Castells Papers.

Patai, Frances. "Mujeres voluntarias estadounidenses en la Guerra Civil española: humanitarias, antifascistas, activistas para la vida." ALBA. Frances Patai Papers. ALBA 131. Series II: Writings. Box 5, Folder 15. ["American Women Volunteers in the Spanish Civil War: Humanitarian, Anti-Fascist, and Activists for Life"].

## Published Works

Abraham Lincoln Brigade Archives. *African Americans in the Spanish Civil War: "This Ain't Ethiopia, But It'll Do"*. New York: G.K. Hall & Co, 1992. [Duncan Collum, Danny (ed.); Berch, Victor A. (chief researcher)].

Aznar Soler, Manuel (ed.). *Barcelona, 11 de juliol del 1937: Segon Congrés Internacional d'Escriptors per a Defensa de la Cultura.* Seville: Renacimiento, 2007.

Bates, Winifred. "A Woman's Work in Wartime." In Jim Fyrth and Sally Alexander (eds.), *Women's Voices from the Spanish Civil War.* London: Lawrence & Wishart, 1991.

Baxell, Richard. *British Volunteers in the Spanish Civil War: The British Battalion in the International Brigades, 1936–1939.* Pontypool: Warren and Pell Publishing, 2007.

Beimler, Hans. *En el campo de asesinos de Dachau: Cuatro semanas en poder de los bandidos pardos.* Barcelona: Ediciones Europa-América, 1937. [*In the Assassin's Field of Dachau: Four Weeks in the Power of the Brown Thugs*].

Bessie, Alvah. "Men in Battle: A Story of Americans in Spain. 1939." In Dan Bessie (ed.), *Alvah Bessie's Spanish Civil War Notebooks.* Lexington, KT: University Press of Kentucky, 2002.

Broggi, Moisès. *Memòries d'un cirurgià.* Barcelona: Edicions 62, 2001. [*Memories of a Surgeon*].

Bullough, Vern L., and Sentz, Lilli (eds.). *American Nursing: A Biographical Dictionary.* Vol. 3. New York: Springer Publishing Co., 2000.

Carrol, Peter N. *La odisea de la Brigada Abraham Lincoln.* Seville: Espuela de Plata, 2005.

Castells, Andreu. *Las Brigadas Internacionales de la guerra de España.* Barcelona: Ariel, 1974.

Celada, Antonio R., González de la Aleja, Manuel, and Pastor, Daniel. *Los Internacionales: English-Speaking Volunteers in the Spanish Civil War.* Barcelona: Warren & Pell Publishing, 2009.

Coale, Robert. "Las Brigadas Internacionales en la Batalla del Ebro." In Josep Sánchez Cervelló and Sebastián J. Agudo Blanco (eds.). *Congreso Internacional sobre la Batalla del Ebro: Ponencias: Vol. I.* Tarragona: Arola, 2011.

Coale, Robert. "The Liberation of Paris, August 25, 1944." *The Volunteer* 36(3) (September 2019).

Crossey, Ciaran. *No pasarán: "We Intend to Show the World."* Belfast: Belfast and District Trades Union Council, 2007.

Derby, Mark, and Lowe, David. "Doug Jolly: New Zealand Surgeon in Spain." *The Volunteer,* July 1, 2018.

Eby, Cecil D. *Comrades and Commissars: The Lincoln Battalion in the Spanish Civil War.* University Park, PA: Pennsylvania State University Press, 2007.

SOURCES

Etchebéhère, Mika. *Mi guerra de España: Testimonio de una miliciana al mando de una columna del* POUM. Barcelona: Alikornio, 2003.

Fisher, Harry. *Camaradas: Relatos de un brigadista en la Guerra Civil Española.* Barcelona: RBA, 2006.

Fishman, Moe. "William 'Bill' Van Felix 1916–2002." *The Volunteer: Journal of the Veterans of the Abraham Lincoln Brigade* 24(4) (December 2002): 20.

Fraser, Pauline. "Felicia Browne: First British Casualty in Spain." *IBMT Newsletter* 37 (July 2014).

Fyrth, Jim, and Alexander, Sally (eds.). *Women's Voices from the Spanish Civil War.* London: Lawrence & Wishart, 1991.

Fyvel, Penelope [Penny Phelps]. *English Penny.* Ilfracombe: Arthur H. Stockwell, 1992.

Gay da Cunha, Jose. *Um brasileiro na guerra espanhola.* Rio de Janeiro: Livraria do Globo, 1946.

Gerassi, John. *The Premature Antifascists: North American Volunteers in the Spanish Civil War 1936–39: An Oral History.* New York: Praeger, 1986.

Green, Nan. "Small Beer." In Jim Fyrth and Sally Alexander (eds.), *Women's Voices from the Spanish Civil War.* London: Lawrence & Wishart, 1991.

Guerra, Francisco. *La medicina en el exilio republicano.* Madrid: Universidad de Alcalá, 2003. [*Medicine in the Republican Exile*].

Güner, Fisun. "Felicia Browne: The Only Known British Woman to Die in the Spanish Civil War." *The Guardian*, July 20, 2016.

Harris Smith, Richard. OSS: *The Secret History of America's First Central Intelligence Agency.* Berkeley, CA: University of California Press, 1972.

Harsányi, Iván. "La participación de húngaros en las Brigadas Internacionales en retrospectiva histórica." In Manuel Requena Gallego and Matilde Eiroa (eds.), *Al lado del gobierno republicano: Los brigadistas de Europa del Este en la Guerra Civil española.* Cuenca: Ediciones de la Universidad de Castilla-La Mancha, 2009. ["The Participation of Hungarians in the International Brigades in Historical Perspective." In Manuel Requena Gallego and Matilde Eiroa (eds.), *With the Republican Government: The Brigadistes of Eastern Europe in the Spanish Civil War*].

Hughes, Langston. *Escritos sobre España (Writings on Spain).* Poems translated by Maribel Cruz and prose by Javier Lucini. Madrid: La Oficina-BAAM, 2011. [Translations of articles, interviews, profiles, and poems written by Langston Hughes about his time as a correspondent in the Civil War].

Jackson, Angela. *Las mujeres británicas y la Guerra Civil española*. Valencia: Publicacions de la Universitat de València, 2010. [Angela Jackson, *British Women and the Spanish Civil War*. London: Routledge, 2002].

Jackson, Angela. *Més enllà del camp de batalla: Testimoni, memòria i record d'una cova hospital en la Guerra Civil espanyola*. Valls: Cossetània, 2004. [*Beyond the Battlefield: Testimony, Memory and Remembrance of a Cave Hospital in the Spanish Civil War*. Pontypool: Warren & Pell, 2005].

Jackson, Angela. *Para nosotros era el cielo: Pasión, dolor y fortaleza de Patience Darton: De la Guerra Civil española a la China de Mao*. Barcelona: Ediciones San Juan de Dios, Campus Docent, 2012. [*'For Us It Was Heaven': The Passion, Grief and Fortitude of Patience Darton: From the Spanish Civil War to Mao's China*, Brighton: Sussex Academic Press, 2012].

Jirku, Gusti. ¡Nosotras estamos con vosotros! Mujeres antifascistas de distintos países hablan de su trabajo en España. Madrid: AABI. [*We Women Are With You! Antifascist Women from Different Countries Talk About Their Work in Spain*. There is currently no English translation].

Jump, Jim, Díez, Antonio, and González, David (eds.). *Hablando de leyendas: Poemas para España: Poemas escritos por brigadistas internacionales de las Islas Británicas que participaron en la Guerra Civil Española*. Tenerife: Baile del Sol, 2009. [*Speaking of Legends: Poems for Spain: Poems Written by Members of the International Brigade from the British Isles Who Participated in the Spanish Civil War*. There is currently no English translation].

Landis, Arthur. *The Abraham Lincoln Brigade*. New York: Citadel Press, 1968.

MacDougall, Ian (ed.). *Voices from the Spanish Civil War: Personal Recollections of Scottish Volunteers in Republican Spain 1936–39*. Edinburgh: Polygon, 1986.

Manning, Leah. "The Cave by the River." In Jim Fyrth and Sally Alexander (eds.), *Women's Voices from the Spanish Civil War*. London: Lawrence & Wishart, 1991.

Martin, Sylvia. *Ink in Her Veins: The Troubled Life of Aileen Palmer*. Perth, WA: UWA Publishing, 2016.

Mora, Juan Miguel de. *La libertad, Sancho...: Testimonio de un soldado de las Brigadas Internacionales*. Cuenca: Ediciones de la Universidad de Castilla-La Mancha; Libros para Todos, 2008. [*Freedom, Sancho...: Testimony of a Soldier in the International Brigades*. There is currently no English translation].

Murray, Annie. "I Shall Never Forget." In Jim Fyrth and Sally Alexander (eds.), *Women's Voices from the Spanish Civil War*. London: Lawrence & Wishart, 1991.

O'Riordan, Michael. *Connolly Column: The Story of the Irishmen Who Fought in the Ranks of the International Brigades in the National-Revolutionary War of the Spanish People, 1936–1939.* Torfaen: Warren & Pell Publishing, 2005.

Patai, Frances. "Heroines of the Good Fight: Testimonies of U.S. Volunteer Nurses in the Spanish Civil War, 1936–1939." *Nursing History Review: Official Journal of the American Association for the History of Nursing* 3 (1995): 76–104.

Perucho, Arturo. *Hans Beimler.* Barcelona: Maucci, c.1936.

Phillips, Nancy, Weber, Georgia, and Vogel, Lise. "Las mujeres americanas y la Guerra Civil española." Asociación de Amigos de las Brigadas Internacionales. www.brigadasinternacionales.org. ["American Nurses Spain," a paper written by Nancy Phillips, Georgia Weber, and Lise Vogel of Friends and Families of the Abraham Lincoln Brigade, and read at the symposium "Solidarias" ("Women in Solidarity") held in October 2018 in Paris].

Preston, Paul. *Idealistes sota les bales: Històries de la Guerra Civil.* Barcelona: Proa, 2007. [*Idealists Under Fire: Stories of the Civil War.* This is a Catalan edition; the Spanish and English editions were published in 2008. The English edition: *We Saw Spain Die: Foreign Correspondents in the Spanish Civil War* (London: Constable and Robinson, 2008)].

Preston, Paul. "Dos médicos y una causa: Len Crome y Reginald Saxton en las Brigadas Internacionales." *Ayer: Revista de Historia Contemporánea, núm. 56: Las Brigadas Internacionales.* Madrid: Asociación de Historia Contemporánea; Marcial Pons, 2004. ["Two Doctors and One Cause: Len Crome and Reginald Saxton in the International Brigades." *International Journal of Iberian Studies* 19(1): 5–24. ISSN 1364-971X].

Requena Gallego, Manuel, and Sepúlveda Losa, Rosa M. *La sanidad en las Brigadas Internacionales.* Cuenca: Ediciones de la Universidad de Castilla-La Mancha, 2006.

Rolfe, Edwin. *The Lincoln Battalion: The Story of the Americans Who Fought in Spain in the International Brigades.* New York: VALB, 1939.

Sánchez Cervelló, Josep (ed.). *El pacte de la No Intervenció: La internacionalització de la Guerra Civil espanyola.* Tarragona: URV, 2009. [*The Non-Intervention Agreement: The Internationalization of the Spanish Civil War.* There is currently no English translation].

Sánchez Cervelló, Josep, and Agudo Blanco, Sebastián J. (eds.). *La Batalla del Ebro: perspectivas y balance: Ponencias.* Tarragona: Arola, 2011. [*The Battle on the Ebre: Perspectives and Conclusions.* There is currently no English translation].

Sartre, Jean-Paul. *Paisatge d'un segle.* Lleida: El Jonc, 2006. [Original collection of essays by Sartre translated into Catalan. No French original exists. No English translation].

Schiborowski, Ingrid. "German Women in the War Against Fascism in Spain 1936–1939." *Kämpfer und Freunde der Spanischen Republik 1936–1939 e.V.* (KFSR), November 24, 2018. www.kfsr.info.

Scholten, Yvonne. "Fanny, Queen of the Machine Gun." *The Volunteer*, December 4, 2011.

Silverthorne, Thora. "The First Medical Unit." In Jim Fyrth and Sally Alexander (eds.), *Women's Voices from the Spanish Civil War.* London: Lawrence & Wishart, 1991.

Skoutelsky, Rémi. *Novedad en el frente: Las Brigadas Internacionales en la guerra civil.* Madrid: Temas de Hoy, 2006.

Solé Sabaté, Josep M., and Villarroya, Joan (ed.). *Breu història de la Guerra Civil a Catalunya.* Barcelona: Edicions 62, 2005. [*Brief History of the Civil War in Catalonia.* There is currently no English translation].

Torriente Brau, Pablo de la. *Cartas y crónicas de España.* Havana: Centro Cultural Pablo de la Torriente Brau, 1999. [*Letters and Chronicles from Spain*].

Torriente Brau, Pablo de la. *Peleando con los milicianos.* Havana: Editora Política, 1987. [*Fighting With the Milicianos*].

Urmston, Lillian. "Across the Ebro." In Jim Fyrth and Sally Alexander (eds.), *Women's Voices from the Spanish Civil War.* London: Lawrence & Wishart, 1991.

Vila, Eloi. *Cartes des del front.* Barcelona: Ara Llibres, 2012. [*Letters from the Front.* A selection from twenty letters and diaries written by Catalans on the front].

Waller, John H. *The Unseen War in Europe: Espionage and Conspiracy in the Second World War.* London: I.B. Tauris, 1996.

Weatherford, Doris. *American Women during World War II: An Encyclopedia.* New York: Routledge, 2010.

Yates, James. *De Misisipi a Madrid: Memorias de un afro-americano de la Brigada Lincoln.* Madrid: La Oficina-BAAM, 2011. [*Mississippi to Madrid: Memoir of a Black American in the Abraham Lincoln Brigade*]. Greensboro, NC: Open Hand Pub., 1988.

## Other Sources

ALBA *Database.* Abraham Lincoln Brigade Archives. https://alba-valb.org/volunteers.

*Le Maitron. Dictionnaire biographique.* http://maitron-fusilles-40-44.univ-paris1.fr/.

Martí-Rueda, Jordi. Entrevista a Juan Miguel de Mora [Interview by the author with Juan Miguel de Mora]. Sitges, Barcelona, October 21, 2008.

*Russian State Archive of Socio-Political History* (RGASPI). http://rgaspi. org.

*Spanienarchiv.* Dokumentationsarchiv des Österreichischen Widerstandes. https://doew.at/erinnern/biographien/spanienarchiv-online.

*The* UKAHN *Bulletin.* The UK Association for the History of Nursing. https://bulletin.ukahn.org.

# List of Photographs

"The Nameless." *ANC/Generalitat de Catalunya (Segona República)/ 1801283/133.*

"The Decision." Mirko Markovics, on the left. *Abraham Lincoln Brigade Archives. Courtesy of the Tamiment Library, New York University.*

"Len Crome." Len Crome. *Courtesy of Peter Crome.*

"Capitana Etchebéhère." Mika Etchebéhère, on the right. *All rights reserved.*

"Silence." Thora Silverthorne, in the middle. Photograph by Vera Elkan. © *Imperial War Museum. HU 71685.*

"The Patient." Walter Garland, on the right. *Archivo Fotográfico AABI.*

"Dr. Jolly." Douglas Jolly, seated on the left, in a blood transfusion truck. Photograph by the Argentine brigadista, Fernando Iaffa. *Courtesy of Máximo Iaffa.*

"George Nathan's Last Wish." Photograph by Vera Elkan. *Imperial War Museum, HU 71638.*

"The Writer Who Didn't Want to Write." Ludwig Renn, on the right. *Bundesarchiv Bild.*

"Hot Water." *ANC/Generalitat de Catalunya (Segona República)/186099/ 1866.*

"Beating the Odds." Bill van Felix, on the left. *Abraham Lincoln Brigade Archives. Courtesy of the Tamiment Library, New York University.*

"Mothers." Esther Silverstein, seated; behind her, to the right, Moisès Broggi. *Courtesy of the Moisès Broggi family.*

"Harry Fisher." Harry Fisher, on the right. *Abraham Lincoln Brigade Archives. Courtesy of the Tamiment Library, New York University.*

"Don't Close Your Eyes." Alvah Bessie. *Abraham Lincoln Brigade Archives. Courtesy of the Tamiment Library, New York University.*

"Ernst Busch." Ernst Busch. *Source: Gedenskstätte Deutscher Widerstand/ Keustxches Kabarettarchiv Mainz.*

"Annie Murray." Annie Murray. *Working Class Movement Library. University of Salford.*

"Erika Glaser." *ANC/Centro Español de Moscú (AGE)/365529/530.*

"Frank Ryan." Frank Ryan, on the left. *Abraham Lincoln Brigade Archives. Courtesy of the Tamiment Library, New York University.*

"Merriman." Robert Merriman, on the right. *Abraham Lincoln Brigade Archives. Courtesy of the Tamiment Library, New York University.*

"The Legend." Milton Wolff. *Abraham Lincoln Brigade Archives. Courtesy of the Tamiment Library, New York University.*

"Jimmy Rutherford." *ANC/Generalitat de Catalunya (Segona República)/186320/2986.*

"The Guerrilla Warrior." Bill Aalto. *Abraham Lincoln Brigade Archives. Courtesy of the Tamiment Library, New York University.*

"Patience Darton." Patience Darton, a short time before leaving for the Peninsula. *All rights reserved.*

"The Irishman." Michael O'Riordan. *Courtesy of Manus O'Riordan.*

"René Cazala's Last Shot." *Abraham Lincoln Brigade Archives. Courtesy of the Tamiment Library, New York University.*

"Valediction." *Abraham Lincoln Brigade Archives. Courtesy of the Tamiment Library, New York University.*

"Fear." Lillian Urmston. *Abraham Lincoln Brigade Archives. Courtesy of the Tamiment Library, New York University.*

"The Man Who Invented Things." Reginald Saxton, working in the cave hospital at La Bisbal de Falset. Photograph by Alec Wainman. © *The Estate of Alexander Wheeler Wainman, John Alexander Wainman (Serge Alternés).*

"Nan Green's Blood." Nan Green with her children a short time before her trip to the Peninsula. *Courtesy of Crispin Green. ANC/Nan Green (AGE).*

"The Heroine." Ruth Davidow, second to the right, on tour in the United States with Evelyn Hutchins (left), a short time after retuning from the Peninsula. *Abraham Lincoln Brigade Archives. Courtesy of the Tamiment Library, New York University.*

"The Hill." Joe Bianca. *Abraham Lincoln Brigade Archives. Courtesy of the Tamiment Library, New York University.*

"Hill 666." Image of the rock that marks the approach to Hill 666, as seen from the highway. *Photograph by Jordi Martí-Rueda.*

"The Last Man." *ANC/Centro Español de Moscú (AGE)/365196/197.*

"A Glass of Wine Before Dying." Hans Landauer during the farewell to the International Brigades in Barcelona. Photograph by Agustí Centelles.

*Ministerio de Educación, Cultura, y Deporte, Centro Documental de la Memoria Històrica, Archivo Centelles, Foto.*2219.

"Braina Voss." Braina Voss in S'Agaró. Photograph by Vicenç Gandol. *Arxiu Municipal de Sant Feliu de Guíxols.*

"Courage." *ANC/Juan Perea Capulino (AGE) /101696/ 80.*

"Write My Name." Jose Gay da Cunha. *Russian State Archive of Social and Political History (RGASPI).*

"The Landless." *Abraham Lincoln Brigade Archives. Courtesy of the Tamiment Library, New York University.*

"Paula Draxler." Paula Draxler, on the right. *Archivo Fotográfico AABI.*

"Frida Stewart." Frida Stewart. *Centro de Documentación de las Brigadas Internacionales.*

"Roberto Vincenzi." *ANC/Generalitat de Catalunya (Segona República)/186973/2229.*

"Where is My Home?" Juan Miguel de Mora. Source: Juan Miguel de Mora, La libertad, Sancho…: Testimony of a soldier of the International Brigades, *Mexico, D.F., Ediciones de laUniversidad de Castilla-La Mancha, Libros para Todos, 2008.*

"Aileen." Aileen Palmer, on the right, with Thora Silverthorne. *Working Class Movement Library. University of Salford.*

"Colonel Fabien." Pierre Georges. *All rights reserved.*

"Rol-Tanguy." Henri Rol-Tanguy, the day Paris was liberated. *All rights reserved.*

# INDEX

note: *ill* refers to an illustration; *port* to a portrait

Thanks to our Patreon subscriber:

*Ciaran Kane*

Who has shown generosity and comradeship in support of our publishing.

Check out the other perks you get by subscribing to our Patreon – visit patreon.com/plutopress.

Subscriptions start from £3 a month.

## The Pluto Press Newsletter

Hello friend of Pluto!

Want to stay on top of the best radical books
we publish?

Then sign up to be the first to hear about our
new books, as well as special events,
podcasts and videos.

You'll also get 50% off your first order with us
when you sign up.

Come and join us!

Go to bit.ly/PlutoNewsletter

PGIL2021USA